JN452533

# Grammar
## Form and Function 1B

Second Edition

# WORKBOOK

Milada Broukal
Amy Parker

Mc
Graw
Hill

**Grammar Form and Function, 2nd Edition 1B Workbook**

**English Adaptation 2011**



Original ISBN: 978-0-07-301198-1

Editorial director: Tina B. Carver
Executive editor: Erik Gundersen
Sr. developmental editor: Annie Sullivan
Editorial assistant: Kasey Williamson
Production manager: MaryRose Bollwage
Cover design: Preface, Inc.
Interior design: Preface, Inc.
Art: Eldon Doty, Preface, Inc.

**Photo credits:**
All photos are courtesy of Getty Images Royalty-Free Collection.



8 9 0 Artec 20 25

When ordering this title, please use

ISBN 10: 89-6055-198-8
ISBN 13: 978-89-6055-198-5

Printed in Korea

# Contents

## UNIT 10 OBJECTS AND PRONOUNS



## UNIT 11 MODALS



## UNIT 12 SPECIAL EXPRESSIONS

## UNIT 13 ADJECTIVES AND ADVERBS



## UNIT 14 THE PRESENT PERFECT

# UNIT 8
# THE FUTURE

## 8a The Future with *Be Going To*

Student Book p. 210

### 1 Practice

**Complete the sentences with the correct form of *be going to*.**

1. Jose ___is going to___ go to the Philippines next summer.
2. Amy __________ meet him there.
3. They __________ get married.
4. Then they __________ travel to Hawaii.
5. Jose __________ work in Japan.
6. Amy __________ teach English there.
7. They (not) __________ have children right away.
8. They __________ stay in Japan for five years.
9. They (not) __________ buy a house.
10. I __________ visit them next year.
11. I (not) __________ stay very long.
12. They __________ be happy together.

### 2 Practice

**Complete the conversations with *be going to* and the verbs in parentheses.**

**A.** A: What (do) ___are___ (1) you ___going to do___ (1) this weekend?

B: I (not, do) __________ (2) anything. I (stay) __________ (3) in bed, and I (sleep) __________ (4) a lot. What (do) __________ (5) you __________ (5)?

A: I (see) __________ (6) a movie. After that, I (eat) __________ (7) Indian food.

**B.** A: Why are you smiling?

B: I (go) __________ (1) to Paris for four days.

A: Four days? Why?

B: I (visit) ___2___ some friends. They (get) ___3___ married.

A: That's great!

B: Yes, and I (stay) ___4___ at their house, and they (buy) ___5___ my ticket.

A: You're lucky!

## 3 Practice

**Write predictions using *be going to* and a phrase from the list. Use contractions when possible.**

| | | |
|---|---|---|
| buy some flowers | have a dinner party | rain |
| call a friend | not get up | ride her bike |
| eat his lunch | not take the bus | take a test tomorrow |
| go on vacation | order a pizza | |

**1.** Patrick has a sandwich.

*He's/Patrick's going to eat his lunch*.

**2.** Sheri is putting on her helmet.

______________________________.

**3.** David is looking at a pizza menu.

______________________________.

**4.** Tim turned off his alarm.

______________________________.

**5.** Carrie is picking up her phone.

______________________________.

**6.** Sue and Carol are taking money out of their wallets.

______________________________.

**7.** Maria is waiting for a taxi and carrying a suitcase.

______________________________.

**8.** Walter is studying.

______________________________.

**9.** Roberto bought a lot of food!

______________________________.

10. Min is taking his umbrella.

________________________________________.

11. Sandra is picking up her car keys.

________________________________________.

## 4 Practice

**Write about what you are going to do or are not going to do on your next vacation.**

1. study

   *I'm not going to study on my vacation*.

2. wake up early

   ________________________________________.

3. take photos

   ________________________________________.

4. visit a friend

   ________________________________________.

5. send postcards

   ________________________________________.

6. swim in the ocean

   ________________________________________.

7. read the paper

   ________________________________________.

8. leave the country

   ________________________________________.

9. email friends

   ________________________________________.

10. speak English

    ________________________________________.

## 5 Practice

**Your friend is going to open a new restaurant. Use the prompts to write questions. Write your own answers.**

1. when/it/open

   *When is it going to open*?

   *Next Wednesday*.

2. what/kind of food/it have

________________________________________?

________________________________________.

3. how many/people/work there

________________________________________?

________________________________________.

4. where/it/be

________________________________________?

________________________________________.

5. what/waiters/wear

________________________________________?

________________________________________.

6. when/you/quit/your job

________________________________________?

________________________________________.

## 8b Future Time Expressions

Student Book p. 215

### 6 Practice

**Write about your future plans. Use time expressions and *be going to*.**

1. Next winter, ______________________________.
2. In a couple years, ______________________________.
3. In 15 minutes, ______________________________.
4. A week from today, ______________________________.
5. Next weekend, ______________________________.
6. Tomorrow morning, ______________________________.
7. Tonight, ______________________________.

8. In three weeks, ______________________________.

9. In two hours, ______________________________.

10. After school next Monday, ______________________________.

## 7 Practice

**Complete the following sentences. Use *tomorrow, next, in, yesterday, last,* and *ago*.**

1. Renata and Claudia met six years ____ago____.
   Now, they go on vacation together.
2. ______________ year, they went to Bali.
3. ______________, they left for Mexico.
4. ______________, they are going to go to the beach.
5. ______________ five days, they're going to visit Mexico City.
6. ______________ week, they're going to take a tour.
7. They're going to come back ______________ two weeks.
8. They decided to go on this trip three months ______________.
9. ______________ month, they bought their tickets.

## 8 Practice

**Write *C* beside the sentence if *tomorrow, next, in, yesterday, last,* or *ago* are used correctly. Write *I* if *tomorrow, next, in, yesterday, last,* or *ago* are used incorrectly.**

__I__ 1. They got married next week.

_____ 2. Karina is going to take her driver's test two days ago.

_____ 3. We're going to the museum tomorrow.

_____ 4. What did you do in 10 minutes ago?

_____ 5. Where is he going to be yesterday?

_____ 6. Ronaldo didn't come with us last week.

_____ 7. Four years ago, Deborah was living in Atlanta.

_____ 8. Yutaka is going to study art next semester.

_____ **9.** In 30 minutes, class is going to finish.

_____ **10.** A week ago, I'm going to move to a new apartment.

## 8c The Present Progressive as the Future

Student Book p. 217

### 9 Practice

**A. Andy is going to college. Write about what he is doing this Thursday. Write sentences using the present progressive for the future.**

| Time | Activity |
|---|---|
| 9:00 | arrive at dorm |
| 9:30 | meet roommate |
| 9:30 – 10:00 | put clothes away |
| 12:00 – 1:00 | have lunch with other students |
| 1:00 – 2:00 | tour campus |
| 2:00 – 3:00 | meet with advisor |
| 3:00 – 4:00 | choose classes |
| 5:00 | go back to dorm |
| 5:30 – 6:30 | talk with roommate |
| 6:30 – 7:30 | eat dinner |
| 8:30 – 11:30 | attend welcome party |

1. 9:00 *Andy is arriving at his dorm at 9:00*.
2. 5:00 ______________________________.
3. 12:00 – 1:00 ______________________________.
4. 3:00 – 4:00 ______________________________.
5. 8:30 – 11:30 ______________________________.
6. 9:30 ______________________________.
7. 6:30 – 7:30 ______________________________.
8. 9:30 – 10:00 ______________________________.
9. 2:00 – 3:00 ______________________________.
10. 5:30 – 6:30 ______________________________.
11. 1:00 – 2:00 ______________________________.

**B. Write questions and answers about Andy's schedule.**

1. what/time/arrive/at dorm

   What time is Andy arriving at the dorm ______?

   He's arriving at 9:00 ______.

2. who/he/meet/at 9:30

   ______

   ______

3. who/he/have/lunch with

   ______

   ______

4. when/he/choose classes

   ______

   ______

5. what/he/do/5:30

   ______

   ______

6. when/he/go back/to dorm

   ______

   ______

## 10 Practice

**Complete the conversations using the present progressive as a future tense.**

**A.** A: When's your last class?

B: I (take) ___'m taking___ (1) my last test tomorrow at 10:00. Then I (come) ______ (2) back home and (pack) ______ (3) my suitcase. I (catch) ______ (4) a plane at 1:00.

**B.** A: What (do) ______________ you ______________ this summer?
1 (1)

B: I (go) ______________ on vacation with my family for two weeks. Then for
2

six weeks I (work) ______________ part time at my uncle's pizza restaurant.
3

He (go) ______________ to Italy. In August, I (hike)
4

______________ for ten days in national parks with my brother.
5

B: That sounds great.

A: What about you?

B: I (take) ______________ two classes in Chicago this summer. I (stay)
6

______________ with my aunt, and I (not, live) ______________ in
7 8

the dorm.

A: How (get) ______________ you ______________ there?
9 (9)

B: I (fly) ______________.
10

## II Practice

**Write *F* if the statement is in the future. Write *N* if the statement is happening now.**

_____ **1.** I'm going home in two days.

_____ **2.** We're having a good time.

_____ **3.** She's leaving tomorrow.

_____ **4.** The children are making cookies Saturday morning.

_____ **5.** Our class is having a test next week.

_____ **6.** We're not sleeping right now.

_____ **7.** He isn't working at the moment.

_____ **8.** Mark and Eileen are working on the computer.

_____ **9.** Julia and Miguel are going out tonight.

_____ **10.** Are you coming back soon?

# 8d The Future with *Will*

Student Book p. 220

## 12 Practice

**Make predictions for the year 2100. Use *will* or *won't* to complete the sentences.**

1. People ___will___ have disposable clothes.
2. Women __________ shave their heads.
3. People __________ read newspapers.
4. Men __________ wear make up.
5. Cars __________ use gas.
6. Students __________ attend school from home.
7. English __________ disappear.
8. People __________ have homes underwater.
9. Everyone __________ look the same.
10. Men and women __________ need to sleep.
11. People __________ communicate without speaking.

## 13 Practice

**Complete the conversations with the future tense. Use forms of the present progressive, *will,* or *be going to.***

**A.** Stefan: I (get) ______(1)______ lunch right now. Do you want anything?

Adam: Sure. I (have) ______(2)______ a cheese sandwich, or maybe some soup. What (get) ______(3)______ you ______(3)______?

Stefan: I (think) ______(4)______ about pizza.

Adam: Oh, that sounds good. I (have) ______(5)______ pizza too.

**B.** Sandra: I don't feel well.

Gerald: That's okay. I (make) ______(1)______ dinner.

**C.** Jackie: I (go) ______(1)______ home in a few minutes.

Eric: Okay. I (see) ______(2)______ you tomorrow.

**D.** Ginny: What (do) ______ (1) you ______ (1) tomorrow night?

Ed: I (go) ______ (2) to bed early.

Ginny: I (rent) ______ (3) a movie. Do you want to come over? I (pick) ______ (4) you up, and I (take) ______ (5) you home.

Ed: No, thanks. I'm really tired.

**E.** Sachiko: Where (be) ______ (1) you ______ (1) this time next year?

Marcela: I don't know. Maybe I (be) ______ (2) in San Diego, or maybe I (move) ______ (3) to Houston.

**F.** Announcer: The concert (start) ______ (1) at 3:00, but the doors (open) ______ (2) at 2:30. Three bands (play) ______ (3). There (be) ______ (4) a short break at 5:00. The concert (finish) ______ (5) about 7:00.

**G.** Kathy: I really don't understand this exercise.

Sam: I do. I (help) ______ (1) you. I (study) ______ (2) tonight at about 7:00.

Kathy: Oh, thanks. I (call) ______ (3) you then.

**H.** Romero: What (do) ______ (1) you ______ (1) now?

Beth: Nothing. Why?

Romero: Dean, Elizabeth, and I (go) ______ (2) the park in an hour. Do you want to come with us?

Beth: Sure. Oh, I (get) ______ (3) another call. I (call) ______ (4) you right back.

Romero: Okay, I (talk) ______ (5) to you later.

# 8e *May* and *Might*

Student Book p. 224

## 14 Practice

**Complete the conversations using *will* when the speaker is sure. Use *may* or *might* if the speaker is not sure.**

**A.** Kevin: Carolina, you are from Quebec, right? I ______(1) go to Ottawa or Quebec this time next year. I'm not sure. Is the weather good then?

Carolina: It ______(2) be. Sometimes it's warm, sometimes it's cool.

Kevin: I ______(3) take the train, or I ______(4) fly. I don't know now.

Carolina: Do you have a hotel? You ______(5) need a reservation. It's very busy this time of year.

Kevin: Okay, I ______(6) make one tomorrow.

Carolina: And you (not) ______(7) have any language problems. Everyone speaks English.

Kevin: That's good.

Carolina: What ______(8) you do there?

Kevin: I ______(9) visit museums, or I ______(10) take a tour.

Carolina: I'm sure you ______(11) have a good time!

**B.** Patty: ______(1) I have a drink of water?

Larry: Sure.

**C.** Michi: This is a nice restaurant. What are you going to have?

Paula: I don't know. I ______(1) have fish, or I ______(2) have tofu.

Michi: I think the fish sounds good.

Waiter: Are you ready to order?

Michi: Yes, I ______________ (3) have the fish.

Paula: And I ______________ (4) have the tofu.

Waiter: Anything to drink?

Michi: I ______________ (5) have some water, please.

Paula: Me, too.

## 15 Practice

**Underline the correct verbs in parentheses.**

1. I (might go / am going) to the doctor's tomorrow. I have an appointment.
2. I (might shop / am shopping). I don't know now.
3. I (might meet / am meeting) a friend for lunch. We have a reservation at 1:00.
4. We (might go / are going to go) to a movie. We bought our tickets yesterday.
5. She (might come / is coming) to my house later. I don't know now.
6. I ('ll be / might be) home at 6:00. We eat dinner then.
7. My husband (will read / might read) the children a story. Sometimes I do it.
8. The children (will go / might go) to bed at 9:00 because it's their bedtime.
9. My husband and I (are going to watch / might watch) a movie. I don't know now.
10. We (will go / might go) to bed around 11:30. We never stay up late.

## 16 Practice

**Write five things you may or might do next weekend. Use ideas from the list or your own.**

| | | | |
|---|---|---|---|
| eat at a restaurant | go to the gym | shop | visit the library |
| go to a museum | meet friends | stay home | watch TV |

1. *I might shop this Saturday*.
2. ______________________________.
3. ______________________________.

4. ______________________________________________.

5. ______________________________________________.

6. ______________________________________________.

## 8f Future Time Clauses with *Before, After,* and *When*

Student Book p. 227

### 17 Practice

**Joe is going back to Virginia for summer vacation. Underline the time clauses in the sentences about him.**

1. Before he goes home, he'll finish his classes.
2. After he finishes school, he'll buy a ticket to Virginia.
3. Joe will be happy when he goes home.
4. When his parents see him, they will hug him.
5. After he gets home, his friends will call him.
6. He'll see a lot of movies when he's there.
7. After he gets home, he'll get a part-time job.
8. He'll email his friends before he comes back to Los Angeles.
9. Joe is going to ask his girlfriend to visit him before he leaves Virginia.
10. When he arrives, his friends will be at the airport to meet him.

### 18 Practice

**Complete the conversations with the verbs in parentheses. Remember that future time clauses use the simple present tense in the time clause and the future tense in the main clause.**

**A.** Tony: When you (get) ________________ (1) to the party, I (introduce) ________________ (2) you to Sophie. She's nice. You (like) ________________ (3) her. Before you (meet) ________________ (4) her, I (tell) ________________ (5) her about you.

Chris: Okay, thanks. Before I (leave) ______ (6) my house, I (call) ______ (7) you.

Tony: I think everyone (be) ______ (8) here when you (arrive) ______ (9). Do you have the CDs?

Chris: Yes, I (give) ______ (10) them to you when I (see) ______ (11) you.

**B.** Donna: How do I get to your house?

Cesar: First, go down Main Street. When you (come) ______ (1) to the corner, you (see) ______ (2) the library. Turn right. After you (go) ______ (3) two blocks, you (see) ______ (4) my house.

Donna: Okay. I (be) ______ (5) there in a few minutes.

**C.** After I (finish) ______ (1) school, I (take) ______ (2) a trip to Europe. I (see) ______ (3) France, Italy, Spain, Germany, Hungary, and the Czech Republic. After I (return) ______ (4), I (look) ______ (5) for a job. When I (find) ______ (6) a good one, I (make) ______ (7) some money. After I (save) ______ (8) some money, I (buy) ______ (9) a small house. I (have) ______ (10) a big garden in the back yard. I (have) ______ (11) dinner parties every weekend.

## 19 Practice

**Answer the questions.**

**1.** What are you going to do after you finish this exercise?

______________________________________________.

2. What are you going to do before you go to bed tonight?

________________________________________.

3. What are you going to tell your teacher when you go to your next class?

________________________________________.

## 8g Future Conditional Sentences

Student Book p. 230

### 20 Practice

**Match the sentence parts. Then write the sentences.**

| | | | |
|---|---|---|---|
| d | 1. go to college | a. | eyes get tired |
| ___ | 2. drink a lot of coffee | b. | not feel healthy |
| ___ | 3. finish homework | c. | have time for parties |
| ___ | 4. wear a helmet | d. | get a good job |
| ___ | 5. work a long time at the computer | e. | not be late to work |
| ___ | 6. find a part time job | f. | not sleep |
| ___ | 7. get up early | g. | make a little money |
| ___ | 8. not exercise | h. | be safe on a bicycle |
| ___ | 9. not brush teeth | i. | not have any teeth left |

1. If you go to college, you'll get a good job.
2. ______________________________.
3. ______________________________.
4. ______________________________.
5. ______________________________.
6. ______________________________.
7. ______________________________.
8. ______________________________.
9. ______________________________.

## 21 Practice

**Complete the sentences with the correct form of the verbs in parentheses. Sometimes two answers are possible.**

1. We (go) ____________________ to Brazil on our next vacation if we (get) ____________________ cheap tickets.
2. If we (visit) ____________________ the beaches in Rio, we (not, have) ____________________ to go to the Amazon.
3. If we (go) ____________________ to the Amazon, we (visit) ____________________ our friends there.
4. If they (have) ____________________ time, they (join) ____________________ us on a tour of the Amazon River.
5. We (stay) ____________________ with our friends, or we (stay) ____________________ in a hotel. We don't know now.
6. If we (stay) ____________________ in a hotel, we (eat) ____________________ at restaurants.
7. If we (stay) ____________________ with our friends, we (have) ____________________ meals with them.
8. If we (not, go) ____________________ to the Amazon, we (stay) ____________________ in Rio.
9. If we (stay) ____________________ in Rio, we (visit) ____________________ Sao Paulo.
10. If we (have) ____________________ a good time in Brazil, we (come) ____________________ back next year.

# 8h The Simple Present with Time Clauses and *If* Clauses

Student Book p. 233

## 22 Practice

**Match the sentence parts. Then write the sentences using *when, before, after,* or *if* in the time clause.**

| | | |
|---|---|---|
| b | **1.** When you water plants, | **a.** I usually buy a sandwich. |
| ____ | **2.** Before the sun comes up every morning, | **b.** they grow. |
| ____ | **3.** After lunch, | **c.** the river's water rises. |
| ____ | **4.** If you don't open the windows, | **d.** Tom always drinks coffee. |
| ____ | **5.** When I go to the café, | **e.** I go for a three-mile run. |
| ____ | **6.** After it rains, | **f.** the apartment will be too hot. |

**1.** When you water plants, they grow.

**2.** ______________________________.

**3.** ______________________________.

**4.** ______________________________.

**5.** ______________________________.

**6.** ______________________________.

## 23 Practice

**Complete the sentences with main clauses about yourself.**

**1.** If I read the newspaper every morning, I know what is happening.

**2.** If I work out, ______________________________.

**3.** If I don't do my homework, ______________________________.

**4.** If I don't eat breakfast, ______________________________.

**5.** If I work hard, ______________________________.

**6.** If I don't feel well, ______________________________.

**7.** When I cook, ______________________________.

8. When I'm lonely, ______________________________________________.

9. When I'm tired, ______________________________________________.

10. When I have a problem, ______________________________________________.

## 24 Practice

**Complete the sentences with the correct form of the verbs in parentheses.**

1. Ryan has class from 10:00 until 3:00 on Monday and Wednesday. After he (finish) ____________________ class, he usually (go) ____________________ to his part-time job.
2. If he (finish) ____________________ work early, he (meet) ____________________ his roommate Tom in the library.
3. This Tuesday, if he (get) ____________________ up early, he and Tom (run) ____________________ for half an hour.
4. After he (run) ____________________, he (take) ____________________ a shower.
5. If he (have) ____________________ a lot of homework this week, he (study) ____________________ at home.
6. When he (get) ____________________ hungry, he usually (make) ____________________ a sandwich.
7. This Friday, he and his roommate (have) ____________________ a party.
8. A lot of people (come) ____________________.
9. When they (have) ____________________ parties, Ryan (make) ____________________ pizza.

10. If Ryan (not, make) ____________________ pizza for this party, he (buy) ____________________ some other food.
11. If they (not, have) ____________________ any food, everyone (be) ____________________ hungry.
12. Before everyone (arrive) ____________________, Ryan and Tom (clean) ____________________ their apartment.
13. After everyone (leave) ____________________, they (clean) ____________________ their apartment again!
14. If the party (go) ____________________ late, they (not, get up) ____________________ early on Saturday.

## 25 Practice

**Answer the questions.**

1. What are you going to do if you have some time this weekend?

   ________________________________________________________________.

2. What do you do when it rains on Saturday?

   ________________________________________________________________.

3. How do you feel when you do well in your English class?

   ________________________________________________________________.

4. When you go shopping, what do you usually buy?

   ________________________________________________________________.

5. When you don't understand the teacher, what do you do?

   ________________________________________________________________.

6. If you have time today, what are you going to do for fun?

   ________________________________________________________________.

7. When you finish this exercise, what are you going to do?

   ________________________________________________________________.

8. What will you do if you don't have any homework tomorrow?

   ________________________________________________________________.

# SELF-TEST

**A Choose the best answer, A, B, C, or D, to complete the sentence. Mark your answer by darkening the oval with the same letter.**

**1.** Cecile is leaving for New York ________ two hours.

**A.** last (A) (B) (C) (D)
**B.** in
**C.** next
**D.** ago

**2.** Bob was in the hospital ________ week.

**A.** last (A) (B) (C) (D)
**B.** in
**C.** next
**D.** ago

**3.** Tina bought the tickets to Hawaii three months ________.

**A.** last (A) (B) (C) (D)
**B.** in
**C.** next
**D.** ago

**4.** Kelly will call you when she ________ her work.

**A.** is finishing (A) (B) (C) (D)
**B.** finishes
**C.** will finish
**D.** is going to finish

**5.** When I ________ TV, I usually go to sleep.

**A.** will watch (A) (B) (C) (D)
**B.** might watch
**C.** watched
**D.** watch

**6.** ________ you have a headache, take some aspirin.

**A.** If (A) (B) (C) (D)
**B.** Might
**C.** Will
**D.** May

**7.** When Mimi sees her son, she ________ be so happy.

**A.** is (A) (B) (C) (D)
**B.** is being
**C.** is going to
**D.** will

**8.** D. J. ________ a computer class this weekend.

**A.** might (A) (B) (C) (D)
**B.** will
**C.** takes
**D.** is taking

**9.** What ________ at 12:00 today?

**A.** will you (A) (B) (C) (D)
**B.** do you
**C.** are you doing
**D.** are you do

**10.** After Peg ________ up, she has two cups of coffee.

**A.** gets (A) (B) (C) (D)
**B.** will get
**C.** is getting
**D.** is going to get

**B Find the underlined word or phrase, A, B, C, or D, that is incorrect. Mark your answer by darkening the oval with the same letter.**

1. Where were you (A) staying (B) last week (C) ago (D)?

   Ⓐ Ⓑ Ⓒ Ⓓ

2. We're (A) going to (B) be married last (C) six months (D).

   Ⓐ Ⓑ Ⓒ Ⓓ

3. She'll have (A) breakfast before (B) she will leave (C) for work (D).

   Ⓐ Ⓑ Ⓒ Ⓓ

4. If he (A) is going to get (B) the job, he will buy (C) a new laptop (D).

   Ⓐ Ⓑ Ⓒ Ⓓ

5. I'm going to (A) have (B) dinner in two hours (C) ago (D).

   Ⓐ Ⓑ Ⓒ Ⓓ

6. If Todd has (A) a lot of work (B), he stays (C) late at work (D) tomorrow.

   Ⓐ Ⓑ Ⓒ Ⓓ

7. Amada is going (A) to go (B) to Athens on her last (C) vacation (D).

   Ⓐ Ⓑ Ⓒ Ⓓ

8. Yesterday (A), John is (B) going to start (C) his new job (D).

   Ⓐ Ⓑ Ⓒ Ⓓ

9. I might (A) not go (B) to the party (C) with you (D) tonight.

   Ⓐ Ⓑ Ⓒ Ⓓ

10. If they (A) will have (B) time, they'll come (C) to the party (D) with us.

    Ⓐ Ⓑ Ⓒ Ⓓ

# UNIT 9
# QUANTITY AND DEGREE WORDS

## 9a *All Of, Almost All Of, Most Of, Some Of, and None Of*

Student Book p. 244

### 1 Practice

**Look at the picture and complete the sentences with *all of, almost all of, most of, some of, or none of.***

1. ____Some of____ the people are children.
2. ________________ the people are adults.
3. ________________ the adults are men.
4. ________________ the adults are dressed up.
5. ________________ the adults are eating and drinking.
6. ________________ the adults are talking.
7. ________________ the adults are playing cards.
8. ________________ the children are playing.
9. ________________ the adults are sleeping.

### 2 Practice

**Look at the photo and complete the sentences with *all of, almost all of, most of, some of, or none of.***

1. ________________ the students are wearing jeans.
2. ________________ the people are students.
3. ________________ the people are men.
4. ________________ the people are women.
5. ________________ the people have dark hair.
6. ________________ the students are paying attention.
7. ________________ the students are looking at the teacher.
8. ________________ the people are standing up.

## 3 Practice

**Look at the photo and complete the sentences with *all of, almost all of, most of, some of, or none of.***

1. ______________________ the people are in an elevator.
2. ______________________ the people are worried.
3. ______________________ the people are men.
4. ______________________ the people are women.
5. ______________________ the people are wearing suits.
6. ______________________ the people is smiling.

## 4 Practice

**Read about Courtney's birthday party. Circle the correct verb.**

1. All of the presents (is / are) wonderful.
2. Some of the music (is / are) good.
3. Almost all of the people (is / are) dancing.
4. Some of the balloons (is / are) on the floor.
5. All of the food (is / are) delicious.
6. Some of the people (is / are) talking.

## 5 Practice

**Read about the new supermarket. Circle the correct verb.**

1. All of the vegetables (is / are) fresh.
2. Some of the fruit (is / are) from South America.
3. All of the customers (is / are) happy.
4. Most of the cashiers (is / are) new.
5. Most of the coffee (is / are) cheap.
6. Some of the wines (is / are) expensive.
7. Almost all of the cheese (is / are) tasty.
8. All of the shelves (is / are) clean.
9. Some of the bread (is / are) delicious.
10. Almost all of the flowers (is / are) beautiful.

## 6 Practice

**Write about the people on your street. Use *all of, almost all of, most of, some of,* or *none of.***

1. ____________________ work.
2. ____________________ wear suits.
3. ____________________ ride bicycles.
4. ____________________ drive every day.
5. ____________________ have children.
6. ____________________ have pets.
7. ____________________ are nice.
8. ____________________ are married.
9. ____________________ travel a lot.
10. ____________________ smoke.

# 9b *Every*

Student Book p. 247

## 7 Practice

**Rewrite each sentence using *every.***

1. All of the computers work.

   ____________________________________________.

2. All of the students in this school are studying English.

   ____________________________________________.

3. All of the chairs are comfortable.

   ____________________________________________.

4. All of the flowers smell good.

   ____________________________________________.

5. All of the photographs are funny.

   ____________________________________________.

6. All of the Japanese restaurants are delicious.

   ____________________________________________.

7. All the neighbors are nice.

   ____________________________________________.

8. All of the birds are singing.

   ____________________________________________.

9. All of the students are laughing.

______________________________________________.

10. All of the exercises are interesting.

______________________________________________.

## 8 Practice

**Write *C* next to the sentence if *every* or *all* is used correctly. Write *I* if *every* or *all* is used incorrectly.**

_____ 1. Every students have a dictionary.

_____ 2. All the students are intelligent.

_____ 3. Every star is out tonight.

_____ 4. All the window is open.

_____ 5. Every cell phone is off.

_____ 6. Every waiters are wearing white.

_____ 7. All the shoes are dirty.

_____ 8. All the book is good.

_____ 9. Every house on our street is big.

_____ 10. All the players is good.

# 9c *Very* and *Too*

Student Book p. 249

## 9 Practice

**Answer the questions. Use *too* or *very* and adjectives from the list.**

| | |
|---|---|
| cold | short |
| difficult | tired |
| noisy | young |

1. Why can't she sleep? ______________________________.
2. Why is he working so hard on the exercise? ______________________________.
3. Why can't she drive? ______________________________.

4. Why can't she reach the top shelf? ____________________.

5. Why is he staying home tonight? ____________________.

6. Why is she wearing a jacket? ____________________.

## 10 Practice

**Match the sentence parts.**

| | | |
|---|---|---|
| ____ | **1.** The music is too loud. | **a.** I'm going to take a nap. |
| ____ | **2.** Chad is very sick. | **b.** Her photos are wonderful. |
| ____ | **3.** Mimi is very smart. | **c.** He needs to see a doctor. |
| ____ | **4.** This exam is too hard. | **d.** I won't pass it. |
| ____ | **5.** She's a very good photographer. | **e.** I can't go with you. |
| ____ | **6.** I'm too busy. | **f.** I can't pick it up. |
| ____ | **7.** The suitcase is very heavy. | **g.** She always does well in school. |
| ____ | **8.** I'm very tired. | **h.** I can't study. |

## 11 Practice

**Complete the sentences with *too* or *very* and adjectives from the list.**

| | | | |
|---|---|---|---|
| angry | excited | hot | sour |
| cheap | far | large | thin |
| cold | happy | late | thirsty |
| difficult | high | nice | |

1. You can't eat that lemon. It's too sour.
2. I'm going to buy that car. It's ____________________.
3. I need some water. I'm ____________________.
4. I like Rita. She's ____________________.
5. I'm going to put on a jacket. I'm ____________________.
6. I don't want to walk. It's ____________________.
7. Tom can't drink the coffee. It's ____________________.

8. I'm getting married! I'm ______________________________________.

9. You've lost a lot of weight. You're ______________________________.

10. I don't understand the exercise. It's _____________________________.

11. Sue missed her bus. She got up __________________________________.

12. Phil didn't buy that jacket. It's __________________________________.

13. I can't sleep. I'm _________________________________________.

14. Mrs. Brown won't talk to anyone. She's ___________________________.

15. I can't reach the shelf. It's ____________________________________.

## 12 Practice

**Choose the answer that describes you. Circle *a* or *b*.**

1. Do you like to ski?
   **a.** No, it's too cold.
   **b.** Yes, but it's very cold.

2. Can you go out on the weekend?
   **a.** No, I'm too busy.
   **b.** Yes, but I'm busy.

3. Do you understand science?
   **a.** No, it's too difficult.
   **b.** Yes, but sometimes it's very difficult.

4. Do you like cake?
   **a.** No, it's too sweet.
   **b.** Yes, but it's very sweet.

5. Do you like to get up early?
   **a.** No, I'm usually too tired.
   **b.** Yes, but I'm very tired.

# 9d *Too Many* and *Too Much*

Student Book p. 252

## 13 Practice

**Complete the sentences about class problems with *too much* or *too many.***

1. There are ____too many____ students.
2. There are ________________ exercises.
3. There is ________________ homework.
4. There is ________________ information.
5. There are ________________ books.
6. There is ________________ noise.

## 14 Practice

**Complete the sentences about a soccer game with *too much* or *too many.***

1. There were ______________________ people.
2. Jesse ate ______________________ candy.
3. There was ______________________ sun and ______________________ wind.
4. The game took ______________________ time.
5. One team had ______________________ players.
6. The other team made ______________________ mistakes.

## 15 Practice

**Dominic and Julia are discussing a movie. Complete their conversation with *too much* or *too many.***

Dominic: Did you like the movie?

Julia: Not really. There was ______(1)______ violence.

Dominic: Yes, there were also ______(2)______ people there.

Julia: I ate ______(3)______ popcorn.

Dominic: Me, too. And, the tickets cost ______(4)______ money.

Julia: Driving to the theater was difficult. There was ______(5)______ traffic.

## 16 Practice

**Write *C* next to the sentence if *too much* or *too many* is used correctly. Write *I* if *too much* or *too many* is used incorrectly.**

__C__ 1. The teachers have too much work.

__I__ 2. There's too many noise in the city.

_____ 3. I always have too many homework.

_____ 4. There are too many people at the beach.

_____ 5. We ate too much food.

_____ 6. There is too many crime.

_____ 7. That's too much information.

_____ 8. I have too many exercises.

_____ 9. Becky made too much mistakes.

_____ 10. They have too much problems.

## 9e *Too* + Adjective + Infinitive; *Too* + Adjective + *For* + Noun/Pronoun + Infinitive

Student Book p. 254

### 17 Practice

**Rewrite the two sentences as one sentence with the same meaning. Use the "*too* + adjective + infinitive" pattern.**

1. This exercise is difficult. I can't do it.

   This exercise is too difficult to do ________.

2. That watch is expensive. I can't buy it.

   ________.

3. Ray and Norm are worried. They can't sleep.

   ________.

4. My mother is sleepy. She can't watch TV.

   ________.

5. Lee is sad. He can't smile.

   ________.

6. The park is far. We can't walk there from here.

   ________.

7. They were sick. They couldn't finish their dinner.

   ________.

8. My daughters are young. They can't go to college.

   ________.

9. He was busy. He couldn't enjoy his free time.

   ________.

10. They got up late. They couldn't catch their plane.

    ________.

## 18 Practice

**Linda and Sam went on vacation, but they didn't have a good time. Rewrite the two sentences as one sentence with the same meaning. Use the "*too* + adjective + *for* + noun/pronoun + infinitive" pattern.**

1. The weather was hot. Linda couldn't stay on the beach.
   The weather was too hot for Linda to stay on the beach.

2. It was rainy. They couldn't go shopping.
   ______________________________.

3. The wakeup calls were early. He couldn't get up.
   ______________________________.

4. The pool was cold. They couldn't get in.
   ______________________________.

5. The water at the beach was rough. She couldn't swim in it.
   ______________________________.

6. The hotel rooms were small. They couldn't feel comfortable.
   ______________________________.

7. The bed was soft. Sam couldn't sleep in it.
   ______________________________.

8. The bathroom was dirty. She couldn't shower in it.
   ______________________________.

9. The people in the hotel were unfriendly. He couldn't talk to them.
   ______________________________.

10. People spoke fast. He couldn't understand them.

_______________________________________________.

11. The food was spicy. She couldn't eat it.

_______________________________________________.

12. Linda's bathing suit was large. She couldn't wear it.

_______________________________________________.

# 9f Adjective + *Enough*

Student Book p. 256

## 19 Practice

**Norman doesn't like his hotel. Write sentences using *too* and *enough* and the adjectives in parentheses.**

1. The water in the shower (cold). It's not (warm).

   *The water is too cold. It's not warm enough*.

2. The bed is (hard). It isn't (soft).

   _______________________________________________.

3. The view is (ugly). It's not (nice).

   _______________________________________________.

4. The carpet is (dirty). It isn't (clean).

   _______________________________________________.

5. The restaurant is (crowded). It's not (empty).

   _______________________________________________.

**Linda doesn't like her class or her classroom. Write sentences using *too* and *enough* and the adjectives in parentheses.**

6. The room is (cold). It isn't (hot).

   _______________________________________________.

7. The room is (dark). It isn't (light).

   _______________________________________________.

8. The desks are (small). They aren't (big).

   _______________________________________________.

9. The class starts (early). It doesn't start (late).

_______________________________________________.

10. The tests are (difficult). They're not (easy).

_______________________________________________.

11. The class is (long). It's not (short).

_______________________________________________.

12. The subject is (boring). It isn't (interesting).

_______________________________________________.

**Virginia and Maureen are trying on clothes. Maureen doesn't like the jacket. Write sentences using *too* and *enough* and the adjectives in parentheses.**

13. This jacket is (small). It's not (large).

_______________________________________________.

14. It's (expensive). It isn't (cheap).

_______________________________________________.

15. The arms are (short). They aren't (long).

_______________________________________________.

16. The color is (dark). It isn't (light).

_______________________________________________.

17. It's (heavy). It isn't (light).

_______________________________________________.

**Cathy doesn't like the city. Write sentences using *too* and *enough* and the adjectives in parentheses.**

**18.** The city is (noisy). It isn't (quiet).

______________________________________________.

**19.** The streets are (crowded). They're not (quiet).

______________________________________________.

**20.** The people are (busy). They aren't (relaxed).

______________________________________________.

**21.** The city is (big). It's not (small).

______________________________________________.

**22.** It's (dangerous). It isn't (safe).

______________________________________________.

# 9g *Enough* + Noun

Student Book p. 258

## 20 Practice

**Complete the sentences with *enough* + a noun from the list.**

| | | |
|---|---|---|
| classes | paint | soap |
| coffee | police officers | sugar |
| customers | reservations | time |
| money | room in the car | water |

**1.** A: Did you finish the test this morning?

B: No, *I didn't have enough time*.

**2.** A: Did you buy gas for the car yesterday?

B: No, ______________________________________________.

**3.** A: Did the restaurant close last week?

B: Yes, ______________________________________________.

**4.** A: Did Ivan graduate in June?

B: No, ______________________________________________.

**5.** A: Was the flight cancelled last night?

B: Yes, ______________________________________________.

6. A: Can you take all five of us home?

   B: No, ______________________________.

7. A: Why are you yawning?

   B: *Because I didn't drink enough coffee*.

8. A: Why is the lemonade sour?

   B: ______________________________.

9. A: What happened to the garden?

   B: ______________________________.

10. A: Why is the crime rate so high here?

    B: ______________________________.

11. A: Why aren't the clothes clean?

    B: ______________________________.

12. A: Why is one wall yellow?

    B: ______________________________.

## 21 Practice

**Gabe and Cindy are going camping. Complete the sentences with *enough* + a noun from the list.**

| | | |
|---|---|---|
| batteries | food | sunscreen |
| clothes | gas | time |
| equipment | information | water |
| film | matches | |
| flashlights | money | |

Gabe: I have two shirts, a sweatshirt, and two pairs of jeans. Do I have *enough clothes?* (1)

Cindy: I think so. I have the camping stove. Do we have ______ (2) to light it?

Gabe: I'll get some more. Look in those bottles. Is there ______________________________?
3

Cindy: No, we need to get some more. What about meals? Is there

______________________________?
4

Gabe: We have a lot of food. Don't worry. Is the car ready? Do we have

______________________________?
5

Cindy: Yes, but we need more cash. We don't have ______________________________.
6

Gabe: Okay. Do we have ______________________________? I got sunburned last time.
7

Cindy: Yes, we do. It might be dark when we get there. Do we have

______________________________ and ______________________________?
8 9

Gabe: Yes, they are already in the car. I found my camera. Is there

______________________________?
10

Cindy: I'm not sure.

Gabe: Okay. Do we have everything else? Sleeping bags, tent? Do we have

______________________________?
11

Cindy: Yes, I think we've got everything. Do you know where this place is? Do we have

______________________________?
12

Gabe: Yes, I have a map and good directions, so let's go! We want to get there before night. Do we have ______________________________?
13

Cindy: We'll leave in 20 minutes. We'll be fine.

# SELF-TEST

**A Choose the best answer, A, B, C, or D, to complete the sentence. Mark your answer by darkening the oval with the same letter.**

**1.** ________ the dishes come with a salad.

**A.** All of
**B.** Very
**C.** Every
**D.** Enough

Ⓐ Ⓑ Ⓒ Ⓓ

**2.** The suitcase is ________ heavy. I can't lift it.

**A.** all of
**B.** too
**C.** every
**D.** enough

Ⓐ Ⓑ Ⓒ Ⓓ

**3.** He's ________ tired. He needs to see a doctor.

**A.** all of
**B.** very
**C.** every
**D.** enough

Ⓐ Ⓑ Ⓒ Ⓓ

**4.** ________ lesson is interesting.

**A.** All of
**B.** Very
**C.** Every
**D.** Enough

Ⓐ Ⓑ Ⓒ Ⓓ

**5.** That jacket is too expensive ________ Jamie to buy.

**A.** too
**B.** very
**C.** for
**D.** enough

Ⓐ Ⓑ Ⓒ Ⓓ

**6.** Some of ________ are sleeping.

**A.** the child
**B.** the children
**C.** children
**D.** child

Ⓐ Ⓑ Ⓒ Ⓓ

**7.** Min isn't ________ to drive.

**A.** old enough
**B.** old too
**C.** enough
**D.** enough old

Ⓐ Ⓑ Ⓒ Ⓓ

**8.** They didn't have ________ to finish the test.

**A.** time enough
**B.** time too
**C.** too many
**D.** enough time

Ⓐ Ⓑ Ⓒ Ⓓ

**9.** Almost all of the women ________ at the camera.

**A.** is looking
**B.** looks
**C.** are looking
**D.** was looking

Ⓐ Ⓑ Ⓒ Ⓓ

**10.** The bed was ________ cold for her to sleep in.

**A.** too
**B.** very
**C.** for
**D.** enough

Ⓐ Ⓑ Ⓒ Ⓓ

**B Find the underlined word or phrase, A, B, C, or D, that is incorrect. Mark your answer by darkening the oval with the same letter.**

1. [All of the] (A) [men] (B) [is wearing] (C) [hats] (D).

   Ⓐ Ⓑ Ⓒ Ⓓ

2. [Some of] (A) the [music] (B) [are] (C) [new] (D).

   Ⓐ Ⓑ Ⓒ Ⓓ

3. [There were] (A) [too much] (B) [sandwiches] (C) and not [enough drinks] (D).

   Ⓐ Ⓑ Ⓒ Ⓓ

4. [The coffee] (A) [is] (B) [too weak] (C). It's not [enough strong] (D).

   Ⓐ Ⓑ Ⓒ Ⓓ

5. [The food was] (A) [enough greasy] (B) [for her] (C) [to eat] (D).

   Ⓐ Ⓑ Ⓒ Ⓓ

6. [He has] (A) [too much] (B) [problems] (C) and not [enough money] (D).

   Ⓐ Ⓑ Ⓒ Ⓓ

7. [This dinner isn't] (A) [cheap too] (B). It's [too expensive] (C) [for us to eat] (D) here often.

   Ⓐ Ⓑ Ⓒ Ⓓ

8. It's [too difficult] (A) [for me] (B) [pass] (C) the test. I didn't [study enough] (D).

   Ⓐ Ⓑ Ⓒ Ⓓ

9. [Every men] (A) in the room [is working] (B) [hard enough] (C). They're [very] (D) tired.

   Ⓐ Ⓑ Ⓒ Ⓓ

10. [I'm not] (A) [enough tall] (B) [to reach] (C) the window. I'm [too short] (D).

   Ⓐ Ⓑ Ⓒ Ⓓ

# UNIT 10
# OBJECTS AND PRONOUNS

## 10a Object Pronouns

Student Book p. 268

### 1 Practice

**Rewrite the sentences. Replace the underlined words in each sentence with an object pronoun.**

1. Danny loves his new car.

   Danny loves it ____________________.

2. Tara ate the oranges.

   ____________________.

3. I don't know his phone number.

   ____________________.

4. I'm going on vacation with my son.

   ____________________.

5. Jay is talking to his wife.

   ____________________.

6. I put the shoes next to the chair.

   ____________________.

7. We did the homework in class.

   ____________________.

8. They named their daughter Madelyn.

   ____________________.

9. Christine is calling her boyfriend.

   ____________________.

10. Fernando didn't see the movie.

    ____________________.

## 2 Practice

**Rewrite the sentences. Replace the underlined words in each sentence with an object pronoun.**

1. Jana is reading <u>the story</u>.

   Jana is reading it ____________________.

2. She's reading the story to <u>the children</u>.

   ____________________.

3. The children love <u>Jana</u>.

   ____________________.

4. Jana's husband, Louis, drives <u>a city bus</u>.

   ____________________.

5. Louis drives <u>Jana</u> to work every morning.

   ____________________.

6. Louis takes <u>people</u> to work.

   ____________________.

7. People enjoy riding <u>the bus</u>.

   ____________________.

8. Jana and Louis bought <u>a new house</u> last year.

   ____________________.

9. They planted a lot of <u>trees</u> in the yard.

   ____________________.

10. We like <u>Jana and Louis</u> very much.

    ____________________.

## 3 Practice

**Rewrite the sentences. Replace the underlined words with subject or object pronouns.**

1. <u>Fran</u> is my sister.

   She is my sister ____________________.

2. She works on <u>a computer</u>.

   ____________________.

3. She and I are twins.

________________________________.

4. Fran, my friend Ann, and I have dance class on Saturday.

________________________________.

5. The teacher teaches Fran, Ann, and me.

________________________________.

6. Mrs. Jordan and Mr. Byrd are our teachers.

________________________________.

7. We like Mrs. Jordan.

________________________________.

8. Mr. Byrd teaches ballet.

________________________________.

9. We admire Mr. Byrd.

________________________________.

10. He is very patient with all the students.

________________________________.

## 4 Practice

**Rewrite the sentences. Replace the underlined words with subject or object pronouns.**

1. Helen works with three women.

   *Helen works with them*.

2. They ride bicycles to work.

   ________________________________.

3. Helen invited my friends and me to her house for dinner.

   ________________________________.

4. The dinner is on Friday.

   ________________________________.

5. We're going to give Helen some flowers.

   ________________________________.

6. She will love the flowers.

______________________________.

7. Helen is going to make pasta.

______________________________.

8. Derek is going to make a salad.

______________________________.

9. We'll help Derek.

______________________________.

10. When we finish dinner, we'll thank Helen and Derek.

______________________________.

## 5 Practice

**Complete the sentences with the correct pronouns.**

**A.** My brother, Michael, watches too much TV. ___It___(1)'s on all the time. Most of his friends watch ________(2), too. ________(3) doesn't get enough exercise. My parents are worried about ________(4). ________(5) tell Michael to go outside, but he usually doesn't. Michael isn't doing well in his classes. He's not going to pass ________(6). I love my brother. He told ________(7) he isn't happy, and I'm sad about this.

**B.** My girlfriend is in Russia. I miss ________(1) very much. ________(2) is a happy person. ________(3) call her every week, and ________(4) writes email to me every day. ________(5) are going to get married in two years. We'll live with my parents for six months, but we don't want to stay with ________(6) for a long time.

# 10b Indirect Objects

Student Book p. 272

## 6 Practice

**Underline the direct object and circle the indirect object in each sentence.**

1. My father gave 20 dollars to us.
2. Ricardo lent the book to DeeDee.
3. My wife sent the letter to our daughter.
4. Mom passed the pasta to me.
5. We told the story to the police.
6. My husband passed the box to me.
7. I showed the present to him.
8. My best friend emailed the joke to me.
9. Who mailed the package to the school?
10. They sent a postcard to us from their vacation.
11. I handed the papers back to the class.
12. Luke told the secret to us.
13. Hannah sent the cookies to the boys.
14. The bank lent the money to my parents.
15. My mother gave the photos to us.
16. I handed the flowers to her.
17. She gave the information to us.
18. I gave the toys to you.

## 7 Practice

**Rewrite the sentences from Practice 6 to change the position of the indirect object. The sentences should have the same meaning. Do not use *to*.**

1. My father gave us 20 dollars.
2. ______.
3. ______.
4. ______.

5. ______________________________________________.

6. ______________________________________________.

7. ______________________________________________.

8. ______________________________________________.

9. ______________________________________________?

10. ______________________________________________.

11. ______________________________________________.

12. ______________________________________________.

13. ______________________________________________.

14. ______________________________________________.

15. ______________________________________________.

16. ______________________________________________.

17. ______________________________________________.

18. ______________________________________________.

## 8 Practice

**There is a bad phone connection. Ron has to repeat what he says. Underline the direct objects. Then change the direct objects to pronouns and rewrite the sentences using *to*.**

**1.** Ron: Dad lent Steve the car.

John: Who did he lend it to?

Ron: *He lent it to Steve.*

**2.** Ron: Steve showed his friends the car.

John: Who did he show it to?

Ron: ______________________________________________.

3. Ron: Steve's friends gave him a present.

   John: Who gave it to him?

   Ron: ______________________________.

4. Ron: His girlfriend mailed him a card.

   John: Who mailed it to him?

   Ron: ______________________________.

5. Ron: He showed me the card.

   John: Who did he show it to?

   Ron: ______________________________.

## 9 Practice

**Underline the direct objects. Then change the direct objects to pronouns and rewrite the sentences using *to*.**

1. I wrote my best friend a letter.

   I wrote it to my best friend.

2. She sent me a present.

   ______________________________.

3. I showed my sister the present. It was a sweater.

   ______________________________.

4. My sister told me a story.

   ______________________________.

5. I lent my sister the sweater.

   ______________________________.

6. My sister gave me back the sweater.

   ______________________________.

7. She lent me $15.00.

   ______________________________.

## 10c Indirect Objects with *For*

Student Book p. 275

### 10 Practice

**Pamela is sick. Complete the sentences about her family with *to* or *for*.**

1. Pam's husband is going to fix the door ___for___ her.
2. Her husband is going to prepare dinner ______ her.
3. Her son passed the orange juice ______ her.
4. Her daughter is going to open a window ______ her.
5. He's going to give the aspirin ______ her.
6. Her daughter is going to answer the phone ______ her.

### 11 Practice

**You don't feel well. Make requests of your best friend. Use *for* and the prompts.**

1. buy/flowers

   ___Could you buy some flowers for me___?
2. get/homework

   ______?
3. open/door

   ______?
4. prepare/soup

   ______?
5. answer/phone

   ______?
6. get/water

   ______?

### 12 Practice

**You're planning a party. Write sentences using *to* or *for* and the prompts.**

1. email/invitations/friends

   ___We're going to email invitations to our friends___.

2. prepare/food/party

_______________________________________________.

3. open/door/guests

_______________________________________________.

4. offer/drinks/friends

_______________________________________________.

5. show/video of our vacation/guests

_______________________________________________.

6. play/music/guests

_______________________________________________.

# 10d Indirect Objects with Certain Verbs

Student Book p. 277

## 13 Practice

**Mr. and Mrs. Daniels's house caught on fire. Everyone is okay, but they need some things. Their neighbors are helping. Complete the sentences with the words in parentheses.**

1. Don bought (some food/them).

   Don bought some food for them.

2. I made (some bread/them).

   _______________________________________________.

   _______________________________________________.

3. My mom offered (our living room/them).

   _______________________________________________.

4. My sister got (some clothes/children).

   _______________________________________________.

5. The firefighters explained (the cause of the fire/Mrs. Daniels).

   _______________________________________________.

6. When the fire started, my dad called 911. The operator repeated (the address/him)

_______________________________________________.

7. They saved the computer, but it doesn't work. My brother's going to fix (it/them).

_______________________________________________.

## 14 Practice

**Read the sentences. Circle *to* or *for*.**

1. I got a new radio (to / for) my brother.
2. We made a cake (to / for) our class.
3. They explained the rules (to / for) the children.
4. Rudy got flowers (to / for) his girlfriend.
5. My uncle introduced my mother (to / for) my father.
6. Sheldon bought a new car (to / for) his mother.
7. She repeated the address (to / for) the pizza company.
8. Mr. Miller explained the homework (to / for) us.
9. My son made a birthday card (to / for) me.
10. The police repeated the instructions (to / for) us.

## 15 Practice

**Tammy and David went out, and their 14-year-old daughter stayed home with her younger brother. Write sentences using *to* or *for* and the prompts.**

1. Tammy and David/explain/rules/daughter

   Tammy and David explained the rules to their daughter.

2. They/show/emergency numbers/her

______________________________________________.

3. They/explain/bedtimes/her

______________________________________________.

4. David/make/reservations/them

______________________________________________.

5. Tammy/bought/a new watch/David

______________________________________________.

6. Tammy and David/repeat/instructions/her one more time

______________________________________________.

## 16 Practice

**Katie and William had a new baby. Write sentences using *to* or *for* and the prompts.**

1. William/bought/new suitcase/his wife

______________________________________________.

2. He/open/door/her

______________________________________________.

3. At the hospital, the doctor show/picture of baby/them

______________________________________________.

4. The doctor/explain/procedure/them

______________________________________________.

5. The baby came! Katie/introduced/William/their new son

______________________________________________.

6. William/bought/new ring/his wife

______________________________________________.

7. Katie's sister/got/flowers/her

______________________________________________.

## 17 Practice

**Tanya and Stan moved into a new house. Their next-door neighbor Tim helped them. Write sentences using *to* or *for* and the prompts.**

1. Tim/made/dinner/them

   ______________________________________________.

2. He/show/the town/them

   ______________________________________________.

3. He/introduce/them/other people

   ______________________________________________.

4. Tanya and Stan/wrote/thank you card/Tim

   ______________________________________________.

# 10e Possessive Pronouns

Student Book p. 280

## 18 Practice

**Circle the possessive pronoun or adjective in parentheses.**

1. A: Is that (my / mine) laptop?
   B: No, (you / yours) is in the bedroom.
   A: Are these (my / mine) keys?
   B: No, those are (my / mine). (You / Yours) are on the table.
   Don't forget (your / yours) lunch.
   A: That's (my / mine)? Thanks!

2. A: Is that (your / yours) dog?
   B: No, (our / ours) dog is sleeping in the corner.

3. A: Where did I put (my / mine) coffee?
   B: Is this (you / yours)?
   A: Yes, thanks!

4. A: Where should we have the party?
   B: (My / Mine) house is too small. (Your / Yours) isn't big enough either. Let's ask Diane. Maybe we can have it at (her / hers).

5. A: Who didn't do (their / theirs) dishes?
   B: I did (my / mine) dishes.
   C: I did (my / mine).
   D: Okay, okay, they're (my / mine).

6. A: Is that Harry and Kelly's house?
   B: No, (their / theirs) is yellow and white.
   A: Is it a big house?
   B: Yes, but (our / ours) is bigger.

7. A: My class is really good.
   B: (Our / Ours) isn't. It's too big. Mrs. Kaufman is (our / ours) teacher. (Her / Hers) tests are too hard. Maybe I'll come to (your / yours) class.

8. A: We have (our / ours) tickets. Do you have (you / yours)?
   B: Not yet.
   C: I did, but I lost (my / mine)!

9. I remember his name, but I forget (her / hers).

10. A: These CDs are (our / ours).
    B: No, they're not. They're (their / theirs).
    A: Well, they look like (our / ours).
    B: A little bit, but (their / theirs) are new.

11. A: Hey, stop. That's (her / hers) ice cream.
    B: No it isn't. (Her / Hers) is over there. This is (my / mine).

12. A: What kind of sandwich do you have?
    B: I have cheese.
    A: I have peanut butter.
    B: Do you want to trade? I'll give you (my / mine) and you give me (your / yours).

## 19 Practice

**Complete the sentences with *it's* or *its*.**

1. ___It's___ a beautiful day today.
2. __________ a little cold but sunny.
3. Our tree is losing __________ leaves.
4. The radio is on. __________ music is playing softly.
5. Our tire swing is gently moving on __________ rope.
6. Our house looks nice in __________ new color.
7. __________ 1:30 right now.
8. __________ my favorite time of year.

## 20 Practice

**Complete the sentences with *it's* or *its*.**

1. A: Here's one sock. Where's __________ mate?

   B: __________ on the floor. Hey, __________ time to go.

2. A: __________ not working. What's wrong with this computer?

   B: There's coffee in __________ keys. __________ not a strong computer.

3. A: This cake is delicious!

   B: __________ a family recipe. __________ secret is to put a little coffee in it before you bake it.

# 10f Indefinite Pronouns

Student Book p. 286

## 21 Practice

**Complete the sentences with *something, someone, anything, anyone, nothing* or *no one*.**

1. A: What do you want for your birthday?

   B: I don't want ____anything____. I have enough stuff.

2. A: Is there ____________________ wrong?

   B: No, ____________________.

3. I'm hungry. I didn't have ____________________ to eat all day.

4. We called Jim's house, but ____________________ answered.

5. Mother: What are you eating?

   Son: ____________________!

6. A: Shhhh. ____________________ is coming.

   B: Who is it?

7. A: Turn around. There's ______________ on your jacket.

B: What is it?

A: A piece of paper.

8. Answering machine: ______________ is here to take your call.

Please leave a message.

9. A: ______________ locked the door and I don't have a key.

B: Ask at the reception desk.

A: I didn't see ______________ at the desk.

10. A: There was ______________ on the train this morning.

B: That's because it's a holiday.

11. A: I'm bored. I don't have ______________ to do.

B: You're lucky. I have too much to do.

12. A: What's that? I hear ______________ in the kitchen.

B: I'll go see.

A: Well?

B: It was ______________. I didn't see ______________.

13. A: I'm hot. I want ______________ cold to drink.

B: There's ______________ here. I'll go to the store.

14. I want ______________ sweet, but ______________ too sweet.

15. Theresa is going to France, but she doesn't know ______________ there.

16. Customer: I'll have the soup.

Waiter: Do you want ______________ to drink with that?

Customer: No, thanks.

17. A: Did you have fun downtown?

B: Yes, but I didn't find ______________ to buy.

A: ______________?

**18.** A: There's ________________________ good on TV tonight. Do you want to go out?

B: Sure, but I don't have ________________________ to wear.

A: I'll lend you ________________________ of mine.

**19.** A: Look at that star.

B: Where? I don't see ________________________.

**20.** A: Hey, I think you've got ________________________ from your mom.

B: What is it?

A: It looks like a letter.

**21.** A: There's ________________________ in the window. I see a face!

B: Relax. There's ________________________ there.

**22.** Customer: These are nice. Do you have ________________________ in red?

Sales clerk: I'll look for you.

**23.** A: There are a lot of cars here, but I don't see ________________________ in the store.

B: Maybe it's closed.

**24.** First teacher: I had a bad day at school.

Second teacher: What happened?

First teacher: ________________________ did the homework.

**25.** Doctor: I have good news for you. There's ________________________ wrong with you.

Patient: That's great. Thanks!

**26.** A: Is ________________________ there?

B: Let's go. There's ________________________ here.

**27.** A: Are you ready for dinner?

B: I don't want ________________________. I don't feel very well.

**28.** A: What are you doing?

B: ________________________.

A: Want to come over? We'll think of ________________________ to do.

B: Okay. I'll be there in an hour.

# SELF-TEST

**A Choose the best answer, A, B, C, or D, to complete the sentence. Mark your answer by darkening the oval with the same letter.**

1. Those are _______ shoes.

   **A.** mine
   **B.** his
   **C.** theirs
   **D.** yours

   Ⓐ Ⓑ Ⓒ Ⓓ

2. Jason is talking to _______.

   **A.** her
   **B.** his
   **C.** theirs
   **D.** she

   Ⓐ Ⓑ Ⓒ Ⓓ

3. My father lent his car _______ my brother.

   **A.** her
   **B.** for
   **C.** mine
   **D.** to

   Ⓐ Ⓑ Ⓒ Ⓓ

4. Kevin bought flowers _______ her.

   **A.** her
   **B.** for
   **C.** mine
   **D.** to

   Ⓐ Ⓑ Ⓒ Ⓓ

5. Is that pencil _______?

   **A.** my
   **B.** your
   **C.** their
   **D.** yours

   Ⓐ Ⓑ Ⓒ Ⓓ

6. I didn't see _______.

   **A.** nothing
   **B.** something
   **C.** anything
   **D.** no one

   Ⓐ Ⓑ Ⓒ Ⓓ

7. Our teacher didn't give _______ the tests.

   **A.** we
   **B.** us
   **C.** they
   **D.** my

   Ⓐ Ⓑ Ⓒ Ⓓ

8. _______ is in the room.

   **A.** Anyone
   **B.** Them
   **C.** Anything
   **D.** No one

   Ⓐ Ⓑ Ⓒ Ⓓ

9. What is another way to write the following sentence?
   "The doctor handed Mr. Murphy the book."

   **A.** The doctor handed the book for Mr. Murphy.
   **B.** The doctor handed Mr. Murphy.
   **C.** The doctor handed Mr. Murphy mine book.
   **D.** The doctor handed the book to Mr. Murphy.

   Ⓐ Ⓑ Ⓒ Ⓓ

10. There's _______ in my eye!

    **A.** anyone
    **B.** something
    **C.** anything
    **D.** no one

    Ⓐ Ⓑ Ⓒ Ⓓ

**B Find the underlined word or phrase, A, B, C, or D, that is incorrect. Mark your answer by darkening the oval with the same letter.**

1. I offered (A) the juice (B) for (C) them (D).

   Ⓐ Ⓑ Ⓒ Ⓓ

2. Her car (A) is small (B), but my (C) is big (D).

   Ⓐ Ⓑ Ⓒ Ⓓ

3. Hey, there's (A) anyone (B) at the door (C). Will you (D) get it please?

   Ⓐ Ⓑ Ⓒ Ⓓ

4. That's (A) not yours coffee (B). It's (C) hers (D).

   Ⓐ Ⓑ Ⓒ Ⓓ

5. Here's (A) the shoe (B). Where's (C) it's (D) partner?

   Ⓐ Ⓑ Ⓒ Ⓓ

6. I didn't lose (A) something (B). There's (C) nothing (D) here.

   Ⓐ Ⓑ Ⓒ Ⓓ

7. He made (A) dinner to (B) her (C), and he bought her (D) flowers.

   Ⓐ Ⓑ Ⓒ Ⓓ

8. This apartment is (A) mine (B). It's (C) not your (D).

   Ⓐ Ⓑ Ⓒ Ⓓ

9. We told (A) he (B) the news. The car was (C) his (D).

   Ⓐ Ⓑ Ⓒ Ⓓ

10. When we (A) asked him (B), he didn't say something (C) about it (D).

   Ⓐ Ⓑ Ⓒ Ⓓ

# UNIT 11
# MODALS

## 11a *Can*

Student Book p. 296

### 1 Practice

**Write sentences about yourself with *I can* or *I can't*.**

1. play the guitar

   I can play the guitar______________________.

2. speak Spanish

   ______________________.

3. make bread

   ______________________.

4. drive

   ______________________.

5. walk to school

   ______________________.

6. use a computer

   ______________________.

7. ride horses

   ______________________.

8. ski

   ______________________.

9. cook

   ______________________.

10. fly an airplane

    ______________________.

11. swim

_______________________________________________.

12. cut hair

_______________________________________________.

13. take good photographs

_______________________________________________.

14. do this exercise

_______________________________________________.

## 2 Practice

**Write sentences with *can* or *can't*.**

1. my friend Yungbo/do math well

   My friend Yungbo can't do math well.

2. my father/tell funny jokes

   _______________________________________________.

3. Sarah/use a cell phone

   _______________________________________________.

4. I/walk on my hands

   _______________________________________________.

5. my grandmother/write stories

   _______________________________________________.

6. I/watch my favorite movie many times

   _______________________________________________.

7. Tony/make pizza

   _______________________________________________.

8. my nephew/tell time

   _______________________________________________.

9. David/read Japanese

   _______________________________________________.

10. they/listen to music and read at the same time

______________________________________________.

11. Lauren/make a good cup of tea

______________________________________________.

12. my cousin Sonny/play soccer

______________________________________________.

## 11b Questions with *Can*

Student Book p. 298

### 3 Practice

**Kay is interviewing for a new job. Read the job requirements and then read about Kay. Write questions and answers using the prompts.**

| Kay | Job Requirements |
|---|---|
| types | type |
| uses computers | use computer |
| speaks Korean | speak Arabic |
| never learned to drive | drive |
| loves working with people | work well with people |
| has two young children | travel a lot |
| works hard | sometimes work nine hours a day |

1. A. Interviewer: Can you type ________________?

   B. Kay: Yes, I can ________________.

2. A. Interviewer: ________________?

   B. Kay: ________________.

3. A. Interviewer: ________________?

   B. Kay: ________________.

4. A. Interviewer: ________________?

   B. Kay: ________________.

5. A. Interviewer: ________________?

   B. Kay: ________________.

6. A. Interviewer: ________________________________________________?

B. Kay: ________________________________________________.

7. A. Interviewer: ________________________________________________?

B. Kay: ________________________________________________.

## 4 Practice

**Complete the sentences using *can* or *can't* and phrases from the list or your own.**

| | |
|---|---|
| cook | play sports |
| drive well | sing |
| explain English grammar | swim |
| play games | work well with people |

1. My father can sing very well.
2. My mother ________________________________.
3. ________________ my best friend ________________?
4. My brothers and sisters ________________________.
5. ________________ my teachers ________________?
6. ________________ my classmates ________________?

## 5 Practice

**Write questions and answers about what the following people can and can't do.**

1. teachers

Can teachers write well?

Yes, they can.

2. doctors

________________________________________________?

________________________________________________.

3. cooks

________________________________________________?

________________________________________________.

4. teenagers

______________________________________________________________?

______________________________________________________________.

5. babies

______________________________________________________________?

______________________________________________________________.

6. college students

______________________________________________________________?

______________________________________________________________.

7. the police

______________________________________________________________?

______________________________________________________________.

8. musicians

______________________________________________________________?

______________________________________________________________.

9. artists

______________________________________________________________?

______________________________________________________________.

10. your friends

______________________________________________________________?

______________________________________________________________.

11. your boss

______________________________________________________________?

______________________________________________________________.

12. your neighbors

______________________________________________________________?

______________________________________________________________.

# 11c *Could:* Past of *Can*

Student Book p. 300

## 6 Practice

**Jack is 30 years old. Write sentences about what he can do now that he couldn't do when he was two years old. Use phrases from the list.**

| | |
|---|---|
| pay bills | talk |
| reach tall shelves | tell time |
| read | tie his shoes |
| shave | use a computer |
| stay up late | walk well |

1. *He couldn't pay bills then, but he can now*.
2. ______________________.
3. ______________________.
4. ______________________.
5. ______________________.
6. ______________________.
7. ______________________.
8. ______________________.
9. ______________________.
10. ______________________.

## 7 Practice

**Stephanie is 23 years old. Write sentences about what she can do now that she couldn't do when she was five years old. Use phrases from the list.**

| | |
|---|---|
| cook pasta | go to bed at midnight |
| cross the street alone | take the bus |
| do laundry | travel |
| drink wine | use a bankcard |
| eat spicy food | vote |

1. *She couldn't cook pasta then, but she can now*.

2. ______________________________.

3. ______________________________.

4. ______________________________.

5. ______________________________.

6. ______________________________.

7. ______________________________.

8. ______________________________.

9. ______________________________.

10. ______________________________.

## 8 Practice

**There was a big snowstorm and the Williams family was inside their house for five hours. The electricity was off. Write sentences about what they could and couldn't do. Use phrases from the list.**

| | |
|---|---|
| cook anything | play cards |
| go online | read a newspaper |
| go outside | tell stories |
| light candles | use the microwave |
| make a sandwich | watch any DVDs |

1. *They couldn't cook anything*.

2. ______________________________.

3. ______________________________.

4. ______________________________.

5. ______________________________.

6. ______________________________.

7. ______________________________.

8. ______________________________.

9. ______________________________.

10. ______________________________.

## 9 Practice

**Judy was on a 14-hour flight to Australia. Write sentences about what she could and couldn't do. Use phrases from the list.**

| | | | |
|---|---|---|---|
| meet people | ride her bicycle | sleep | take a shower |
| read | run | smoke | watch movies |

1. She could meet people________________________.
2. ________________________________________.
3. ________________________________________.
4. ________________________________________.
5. ________________________________________.
6. ________________________________________.
7. ________________________________________.
8. ________________________________________.

# 11d *Be Able To*

Student Book p. 303

## 10 Practice

**Read about Denise's experience one night. Change the underlined forms of *can* and *could* to forms of *be able to*.**

I was walking one night when I fell into a big hole. I couldn't see (1) the opening, and I couldn't hear (2) anyone. I was afraid. I couldn't feel (3) one of my feet, but I could find (4) the matches in my pocket. I lit the matches, and I felt better. I started to call "Help!" No one could hear (5) me. I finally slept.

When I woke up, I could see (6) the sky, and I could hear (7) traffic. I called out for help again. Finally, a young man looked down the hole, and he could see (8) me! He said he could borrow (9) a cell phone to call 911. The firefighters came and could get (10) me out of the hole. I was okay.

I still have bad dreams sometimes, and I can't sleep (11) without a light on, but now I can talk (12) about my story.

1. *wasn't able to see*
2. ______
3. ______
4. ______
5. ______
6. ______
7. ______
8. ______
9. ______
10. ______
11. ______
12. ______

## II Practice

**Read about Craig's fishing experience. Change the underlined forms of *can* and *could* to forms of *be able to*.**

I don't like fishing because I can't swim (1). One Saturday, my friends invited me to go with them. I got a fishing license because you can't fish (2) without it. I was in the boat, and I couldn't stay (3) awake because the sun was so hot. Suddenly, I could feel (4) something pull on my line. I looked in the water, and I could see (5) this big, big fish. He was really heavy! I couldn't bring (6) him into the boat. My friends were giving me advice, but I couldn't hear (7) them. I was busy. The fish broke the line and swam away, but now I can tell (8) people about the big fish I almost caught.

1. *am not able to swim*
2. ______
3. ______
4. ______
5. ______
6. ______
7. ______
8. ______

## 12 Practice

**Rachel is 13 years old. Write sentences to say what she can do now, what she could do when she was a year old, and what she will be able to do when she's 21.**

| One year | Now (age 13) | Age 21 |
|---|---|---|
| laugh | go to junior high school | vote |
| sit up | take care of her brothers | ski |
| crawl | play the guitar | go to college |
| drink milk | go out with her friends | get an apartment |

1. When she was a year old, *she could laugh* (OR) *she was able to laugh*.
2. Now, ______________________________.
3. At age 21, ______________________________.
4. When she was a year old, ______________________________.
5. Now, ______________________________.
6. At age 21, ______________________________.
7. When she was a year old, ______________________________.
8. Now, ______________________________.
9. At age 21, ______________________________.
10. When she was a year old, ______________________________.
11. Now, ______________________________.
12. At age 21, ______________________________.

## 13 Practice

**Tim is 32 years old. Write sentences to say what he can do now, what he could do when he was five years old, and what he will be able to do when he's 65.**

| Five years | Now (age 32) | Age 65 |
|---|---|---|
| take naps every day | have children | stop working |
| say the alphabet | get married | play with his grandchildren |
| read his name | buy a house | play golf |
| start school | learn English at night | travel |

1. When he was five years old, *he could take naps every day*
   (OR) *he was able to take naps every day*.
2. Now, ______________________________
   ______________________________.
3. At age 65, ______________________________
   ______________________________.
4. When he was five years old, ______________________________
   ______________________________.
5. Now, ______________________________
   ______________________________.
6. At age 65, ______________________________
   ______________________________.
7. When he was five years old, ______________________________
   ______________________________.
8. Now, ______________________________
   ______________________________.
9. At age 65, ______________________________
   ______________________________.
10. When he was five years old, ______________________________
    ______________________________.

11. Now, ______________________________________________

______________________________________________.

12. At age 65, ______________________________________________

______________________________________________.

# 11e *Should*

Student Book p. 307

## 14 Practice

**Richard is moving into his first apartment. Complete the sentences with *should* or *shouldn't*.**

1. He ____________________ pay rent on time.
2. He ____________________ be noisy.
3. He ____________________ have big parties.
4. He ____________________ meet the other people in the building.
5. He ____________________ talk to his roommate about money before they move in together.
6. They ____________________ decide how to divide the housework.

## 15 Practice

**Beverly wants to lose weight. Complete the sentences with *should* or *shouldn't*.**

1. She ____________________ talk to a doctor first.
2. She ____________________ exercise.
3. She ____________________ eat late at night.
4. She ____________________ drink a lot of alcohol.
5. She ____________________ healthy food.
6. She ____________________ eat breakfast.

## 16 Practice

**Laura is a lonely student. Write sentences with *should* or *shouldn't*.**

1. She doesn't smile.

   She should smile ______.

2. She stays home.

   ______.

3. She doesn't call her classmates.

   ______.

4. She is unfriendly.

   ______.

5. She doesn't listen to others.

   ______.

6. She doesn't invite people to her house.

   ______.

7. She doesn't look at people.

   ______.

8. She doesn't ask people about their interests.

   ______.

## 17 Practice

**Read the situations. Write sentences about what you should or shouldn't do.**

1. You feel sick.

   I should see a doctor. (OR) I should take some aspirin.

2. You're late for class.

   ______.

3. You don't understand the teacher.

   ______.

4. You feel sleepy.

   ______.

5. You cut your finger.

______________________________________________.

6. You don't like your roommate.

______________________________________________.

7. You are homesick.

______________________________________________.

8. You go to a dinner party in the United States.

______________________________________________.

9. You forget your homework.

______________________________________________.

10. You're driving, and you see the police.

______________________________________________.

11. You walk home late at night.

______________________________________________.

12. You don't have enough money.

______________________________________________.

## 11f *Must*

Student Book p. 310

### 18 Practice

**Read the following dorm rules. Complete the sentences with *must* or *mustn't*.**

1. You ______*must*______ turn off your music at 9:00 P.M.
2. You ____________________ paint the room.
3. You ____________________ smoke in the room.
4. You ____________________ cook in the room.
5. You ____________________ be quiet after 11:00 P.M.
6. You ____________________ have guests overnight.

7. You ____________________ have big parties.

8. You ____________________ clean your bathroom.

9. You ____________________ have pets.

10. You ____________________ sign visitors in at the front desk.

## 19 Practice

**Read the following driving rules. Complete the sentences with *must* or *mustn't*.**

1. You ____________________ study for the test.
2. You ____________________ practice driving before you take the test.
3. You ____________________ stop at red lights.
4. You ____________________ drive too fast.
5. You ____________________ wear your seatbelt.
6. You ____________________ drink and drive.
7. You ____________________ drive if you are sleepy.
8. You ____________________ pay attention all the time.
9. You ____________________ talk on your cell phone.
10. You ____________________ look in your mirrors for other cars.

## 20 Practice

**Fred broke his leg last week. Read his doctor's rules. Complete the sentences with *must* or *mustn't*.**

1. He ____________________ stay off his foot.
2. He ____________________ keep his foot up.
3. He ____________________ walk.
4. He ____________________ put ice on it.
5. He ____________________ take aspirin every six hours.
6. He ____________________ stand up for long periods of time.

## 21 Practice

**Read about how to take a photograph. Complete the sentences with *must* or *mustn't*.**

1. You ____________ look through the lens.
2. You ____________ stand one meter away.
3. You ____________ put fingers in front of the camera.
4. You ____________ check the light.
5. You ____________ push the button here.
6. You ____________ open the camera before you finish the film.

## 22 Practice

**Write what you must or mustn't do in the following situations.**

1. before you buy a computer

   You must look at prices.

2. before you live with a roommate

   ______________________________________________.

3. before you get married

   ______________________________________________.

4. before you move

   ______________________________________________.

5. before you have children

   ______________________________________________.

6. before you have a party

   ______________________________________________.

7. before you buy a house

   ______________________________________________.

8. before you go to a job interview

   ______________________________________________.

9. before you run a marathon

   ______________________________________________.

10. before you register for classes

_______________________________________________.

## 11g *Have To*

Student Book p. 312

### 23 Practice

**What do you have to do in your house? Complete the sentences with *have to* or *don't have to.***

1. I ____________________ clean my room.
2. I ____________________ make my bed.
3. I ____________________ do the dishes.
4. I ____________________ do laundry.
5. I ____________________ go grocery shopping.
6. I ____________________ pay rent.
7. I ____________________ make dinner.
8. I ____________________ work in the garden.
9. I ____________________ fix the car.
10. I ____________________ tell my parents where I'm going and when I'll be back.

### 24 Practice

**Mark works in the stock market. Complete the sentences with *has to* or *doesn't have to.***

1. He ____________________ be there on time.
2. He ____________________ work on Saturday.
3. He ____________________ wear a tie.
4. He ____________________ work at the office all the time.
5. He ____________________ be friendly at work.
6. He ____________________ speak other languages.
7. He ____________________ work eight hours a day.
8. He ____________________ travel.

## 25 Practice

**Complete the sentences with *have to/has to* or *don't have to/doesn't have to.***

1. I ____________________ do my homework now. I can do it later.
2. I ____________________ go now. I'm going to be late!
3. They ____________________ to drive. It's too far to walk.
4. We ____________________ drive. We can walk there.
5. She ____________________ pick out CDs for the party. She's the DJ.
6. You ____________________ bring anything. We have everything here.
7. Bessie ____________________ get good grades. She wants to go to a good college.
8. The class ____________________ turn in the assignment tomorrow. It is due next week.
9. Jimmy ____________________ clean his room. It is a mess!
10. Alejandro ____________________ go the store. He doesn't have anything to eat at home.
11. Akiko ____________________ study very hard. She is very intelligent, and she remembers everything.
12. David and I ____________________ go to work now, but we don't want to.
13. You ____________________ wash it in cold water. Never wash it in hot water.
14. We ____________________ work tomorrow. It's a holiday!
15. I ____________________ get new shoes. These are too small.
16. Brenda ____________________ wear glasses. She can see well.
17. My mother ____________________ water the garden. The flowers are very dry.
18. I ____________________ drink something. I'm really thirsty.
19. When ____________________ you ____________________ be home?
20. You ____________________ come to my house. I'll come to yours.

## 26 Practice

**Write questions and short answers using *have to* and information from the chart.**

| Qualities | Waiter | Musician | Engineer |
|---|---|---|---|
| Have a degree | | | x |
| Play the piano and sing | | x | |
| Be friendly | x | | |

1. waiter/have a degree

   Does a waiter have to have a degree ?

   No she/he doesn't .

2. waiter/play the piano and sing

   ______________________________?

   ______________________________.

3. waiter/be friendly

   ______________________________?

   ______________________________.

4. musician/have a degree

   ______________________________?

   ______________________________.

5. musician/play the piano and sing

   ______________________________?

   ______________________________.

6. musician/be friendly

   ______________________________?

   ______________________________.

7. engineer/have a degree

   ______________________________?

   ______________________________.

8. engineer/play the piano and sing

______________________________________________?

______________________________________________.

9. engineer/be friendly

______________________________________________?

______________________________________________.

## 27 Practice

**Write about people in different professions. Use *have to/has to* or *don't have to/ doesn't have to* and phrases from the list.**

| | |
|---|---|
| be creative | prevent crime |
| fly airplanes | think of interesting stories |
| help people understand ideas | treat sick people |

1. teacher

A teacher has to help people understand ideas.

A teacher doesn't have to fly airplanes.

2. police officers

______________________________________________.

______________________________________________.

3. pilot

______________________________________________.

______________________________________________.

4. doctors

______________________________________________.

______________________________________________.

5. artist

______________________________________________.

______________________________________________.

6. writers

______________________________________________.

______________________________________________.

## 28 Practice

**My grandmother often tells us about when she was young. Complete the sentences with *had to* or *didn't have to*.**

1. I ___had to___ walk to school.
2. My mother ________________ work. She stayed at home.
3. I ________________ wear dresses every day.
4. I ________________ help take care of my sisters.
5. We ________________ lock our doors. We felt very safe with our neighbors.
6. My sisters and I ________________ be quiet when guests came over. We couldn't be noisy.
7. We ________________ buy vegetables because we had a big garden.

## 29 Practice

**When Hilary was 14 years old, she took care of other people's children. Complete the sentences with *had to* or *didn't have to*.**

1. I ___had to___ read the children a story before they went to bed.
2. I ________________ stay awake. I could sleep if I felt tired.
3. I ________________ arrive on time.
4. I ________________ make dinner. The children ate before I got there.
5. I ________________ walk home. The parents gave me a ride.
6. I ________________ put the children to bed.
7. I ________________ know the phone number of where the parents were.

## 30 Practice

**Write questions and answers using *have to* and the prompts.**

1. David/work/today

   Did David have to work today ?

   Yes, he did .

2. Lynn/do/homework/yesterday

   ______?

   No, ______.

3. Susan and Lisa/go shopping/last night

   ______?

   Yes, ______.

4. the baby/go to bed/early/Saturday

   ______?

   Yes, ______.

5. Roberto/drive to work/yesterday morning

   ______?

   No, ______.

6. Elena/cook dinner/last night

   ______?

   Yes, ______.

## 31 Practice

**Complete the sentences with things you had to or didn't have to do. Use phrases from the list or add your own.**

| | | |
|---|---|---|
| carry an umbrella | see a doctor | turn off the TV |
| cook dinner | solve a problem | wear sunscreen |
| go to school | study for a test | work late |
| go to the library | take the bus | |

1. Last night, I had to work late. (OR) I didn't have to take the bus.
2. Yesterday, ______.

3. ______________________________ on Saturday.

4. ______________________________ on my last vacation.

5. Last week, ______________________________.

6. ______________________________ last year.

7. ______________________________ two days ago.

8. This morning, ______________________________.

## 11h *May I, Can I,* and *Could I*

Student Book p. 317

### 32 Practice

**Complete the dialogues with *may I, can I,* or *could I* and *you can* or *you can't*.**

1. Friend A: Can I ______________ borrow $10.00?
   Friend B: Sure.
2. Young sister: ______________ go with you?
   Older sister: No, ______________.
3. Friend A: ______________ use your computer?
   Friend B: Yes, ______________.
4. Son: ______________ borrow the car?
   Father: No, ______________.
5. Daughter: ______________ do the dishes later?
   Mother: No, ______________.
6. Customer: ______________ smoke here?
   Waiter: Sorry. There is no smoking in the restaurant.
7. Sales clerk: ______________ help you?
   Customer: No, thanks.
8. Boss: ______________ speak to you?
   Sales clerk: Certainly.

9. Son: ______________ stay at Robert's house tonight?

Mother: Yes, ______________.

10. Customer: ______________ speak with the manager?

Waiter: I'm sorry. She's not here right now.

11. Customer: ______________ have some more coffee?

Waiter: Of course.

12. Son: ______________ watch TV now?

Father: Did you finish your homework this afternoon?

## 33 Practice

**Write questions and answers with *may I, can I,* or *could I.***

1. You don't understand the homework. You want to ask the teacher a question.

   Q: May I ask you a question?

   A: Yes, you may.

2. You are ordering ice cream. You want vanilla and strawberry.

   Q: ______________?

   A: ______________.

3. You want to park your car on a busy street. Ask the police officer if you can park here.

   Q: ______________?

   A: ______________.

4. You want to get a cell phone. Ask your mother.

   Q: ______________?

   A: ______________.

5. You're going out, and you want to borrow your sister's clothes.

   Q: ______________?

   A: ______________.

6. You want to change the TV channel. Your brother is also watching TV.

   Q: ______________?

   A: ______________.

**7.** You want to use your friend's camera on vacation. Ask to borrow it.

Q: ______________________________________________?

A: ______________________________________________.

**8.** You're taking a test, but your pencil is broken. Ask to borrow one from a friend.

Q: ______________________________________________?

A: ______________________________________________.

**9.** You're eating lunch at a nice restaurant. Ask for a table near the window.

Q: ______________________________________________?

A: ______________________________________________.

**10.** You're on a bus. You're cold. Ask a stranger if it is OK for you to close the window.

Q: ______________________________________________?

A: ______________________________________________.

**11.** You don't have enough time to finish the test. Ask for more time.

Q: ______________________________________________?

A: ______________________________________________.

**12.** You want a dog. Ask your roommate.

Q: ______________________________________________?

A: ______________________________________________.

**13.** You're on the bus. Someone puts down a newspaper. Ask to read it.

Q: ______________________________________________?

A: ______________________________________________.

**14.** You want to borrow a car. Ask a friend.

Q: ______________________________________________?

A: ______________________________________________.

# SELF-TEST

**A Choose the best answer, A, B, C, or D, to complete the sentence. Mark your answer by darkening the oval with the same letter.**

**1.** I _______ write with my left and my right hand when I was young, but now I can't.

**A.** could Ⓐ Ⓑ Ⓒ Ⓓ
**B.** should
**C.** have to
**D.** must

**2.** They _______ meet us tomorrow. They don't have other plans.

**A.** could Ⓐ Ⓑ Ⓒ Ⓓ
**B.** didn't have to
**C.** had to
**D.** can

**3.** Rose is still working, and it's 12:00. She _______ go to bed.

**A.** should Ⓐ Ⓑ Ⓒ Ⓓ
**B.** didn't have to
**C.** had to
**D.** was able to

**4.** _______ help you?

**A.** Couldn't Ⓐ Ⓑ Ⓒ Ⓓ
**B.** Didn't have to
**C.** May I
**D.** Must

**5.** When you were a child, what _______ you do?

**A.** could Ⓐ Ⓑ Ⓒ Ⓓ
**B.** didn't have to
**C.** had to
**D.** can

**6.** We _______ eat or drink in the library.

**A.** could I Ⓐ Ⓑ Ⓒ Ⓓ
**B.** mustn't
**C.** am able to
**D.** can I

**7.** Steven _______ wear a suit to work. He has to wear a tie, too.

**A.** must Ⓐ Ⓑ Ⓒ Ⓓ
**B.** could
**C.** had to
**D.** can

**8.** _______ borrow your bicycle?

**A.** Can Ⓐ Ⓑ Ⓒ Ⓓ
**B.** May
**C.** Should
**D.** Could I

**9.** She _______ work. Her family has a lot of money.

**A.** could Ⓐ Ⓑ Ⓒ Ⓓ
**B.** doesn't have to
**C.** can
**D.** must

**10.** You _______ stay in bed. You don't feel well.

**A.** should Ⓐ Ⓑ Ⓒ Ⓓ
**B.** didn't have to
**C.** could
**D.** will be able to

**B Find the underlined word or phrase, A, B, C, or D, that is incorrect. Mark your answer by darkening the oval with the same letter.**

**1.** James must to (A) go now (B), but (C) he can come (D) back tomorrow.

Ⓐ Ⓑ Ⓒ Ⓓ

**2.** We have to (A) take a test (B) tomorrow. But we (C) won't be able to (D) study yesterday.

Ⓐ Ⓑ Ⓒ Ⓓ

**3.** Debbie can't ride (A) a bicycle (B) when she (C) was ten years old (D).

Ⓐ Ⓑ Ⓒ Ⓓ

**4.** A whale (A) can swim (B), but it can't (C) to fly (D).

Ⓐ Ⓑ Ⓒ Ⓓ

**5.** You must (A) should have (B) a passport before you can (C) travel (D).

Ⓐ Ⓑ Ⓒ Ⓓ

**6.** Bill must to (A) get up (B) at 5:30. He has to (C) be (D) at work at 7:00.

Ⓐ Ⓑ Ⓒ Ⓓ

**7.** They have to (A) go (B) to work (C). They (D) can stay home.

Ⓐ Ⓑ Ⓒ Ⓓ

**8.** She should (A) to study (B). She has to (C) take (D) a test tomorrow.

Ⓐ Ⓑ Ⓒ Ⓓ

**9.** They are able to (A) help (B) you. What do you (C) must to (D) do?

Ⓐ Ⓑ Ⓒ Ⓓ

**10.** You aren't able to (A) come (B) with us now, but can (C) you to meet (D) us next week?

Ⓐ Ⓑ Ⓒ Ⓓ

# UNIT 12
# SPECIAL EXPRESSIONS

## 12a *Let's*

Student Book p. 328

### 1 Practice

**Write a response to each statement using *let's* and an expression from the list.**

| | | |
|---|---|---|
| build a fire | have a beach party | play games |
| cook some corn | invite Jesse and Eric | sing some songs |

1. What do you want to do tonight? Let's have a beach party.
2. Good idea! Who should we invite?

   ______________________________.
3. What should we do if it gets cold?

   ______________________________.
4. I'm going to be hungry.

   ______________________________.
5. I think Jesse has a guitar.

   ______________________________.
6. The children will be there.

   ______________________________.

## 2 Practice

**It's Raphael's first day at school. He's talking to his new roommate Pierre. Write a response to each statement using *let's* and an expression from the list.**

meet our neighbors
move the furniture
put some interesting pictures on the walls
talk to an advisor
walk around campus

1. This room is boring.

   ______________________________.

2. The beds are blocking the window.

   ______________________________.

3. I don't know what classes I'm going to take.

   ______________________________.

4. Who lives next to us?

   ______________________________.

5. Where's the cafeteria?

   ______________________________.

## 3 Practice

**Some friends are at a wildlife rescue farm. Write a response to each statement using *let's* and an expression from the list.**

get something to eat
go home now
go see the mountain lions
look at the peacock
read about them
watch the film

1. Here's some information about kangaroos.

   ______________________________.

2. I'm hungry.

   ______________________________.

3. I want to see the big animals.

______________________________.

4. Sam wants to see the peacock.

______________________________.

5. Here is a short film about wildlife rescue.

______________________________.

6. I'm tired. Are you ready to leave?

______________________________.

## 4 Practice

**Write responses to the statements using *let's* or *let's not*.**

1. Here comes the train now!

   Let's run______________________________.

2. The coffee shop is open.

   ______________________________.

3. Tomorrow is Vivian's birthday.

   ______________________________.

4. The TV isn't working.

   ______________________________.

5. I just got a new CD.

   ______________________________.

6. That new action movie starts at 9:00.

   ______________________________.

7. I have a headache.

   ______________________________.

8. Our apartment is too small.

   ______________________________.

9. I'm bored.

______________________________.

10. That street looks dangerous.

______________________________.

11. Those oranges are cheap!

______________________________.

12. Uh oh. We are very late!

______________________________.

# 12b *Would Like*

Student Book p. 330

## 5 Practice

**Complete the dialogues with *would like*.**

1. John: ___Would___ you ___like___ to have dinner with me tonight?

   Julia: Sure.

2. John: I ______________ a table near the window.

   Waiter: Certainly.

3. Waiter: ______________ you ______________ something to drink?

   John: Yes, please.

4. Waiter: ______________ you ______________ soup or salad?

   Julia: I ______________ salad, please.

5. Waiter: ______________ you ______________ rice or a potato?

   Julia: Rice.

6. Waiter: ______________ you ______________ anything else tonight?

   John: No, thank you. I ______________ the check.

7. John: ______________ you ______________ to go out with me again sometime?

   Julia: Yes. I ______________ that.

## 6 Practice

**Write sentences with *would like* or *wouldn't like*.**

1. (yes) Susan/go bowling/Saturday
   Susan would like to go bowling on Saturday.
2. (no) Tom/swim/in the ocean
   Tom wouldn't like to swim in the ocean.
3. (yes) Sidney/run/in the New York City Marathon
   ______.
4. (no) He/take/the test early
   ______.
5. (yes) They/feed/the cat
   ______.
6. (no) She/videotape/the party
   ______.
7. (yes) Georgie/plant/tomatoes in the garden
   ______.
8. (no) Pat and Erin/eat/spaghetti tonight
   ______.

# 12c *Could You* and *Would You*

Student Book p. 334

## 7 Practice

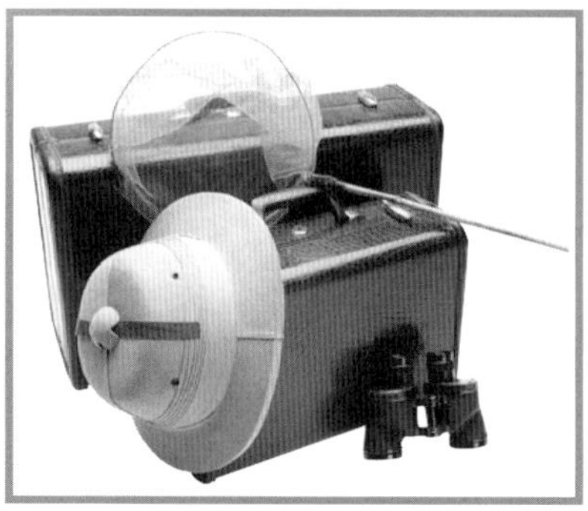

**Benny is going on vacation. He asks his roommate to do things while he's gone. Write his requests using *could you* or *would you* and the prompts.**

1. water my plants
   Could you please water my plants?
2. check my mail
   ______?

3. feed my cat

_______________________________________________?

4. take me to the airport

_______________________________________________?

5. write down my phone messages

_______________________________________________?

6. give the landlord our rent check

_______________________________________________?

7. pick me up from the airport next week

_______________________________________________?

## 8 Practice

**The Lee family is having a dinner party. Christine asks her husband, Joe, and her two children, Will and Lisa, to do things to prepare. Write her requests using *could you* or *would you* and the prompts.**

1. set the table

Lisa, would you please

set the table?

2. clean your bedrooms

_______________________________________________?

3. change your clothes

_______________________________________________?

4. turn off the TV

_______________________________________________?

5. put on some music

_______________________________________________?

6. light the candles

______________________________________________?

7. wash the lettuce

______________________________________________?

## 9 Practice

**Write polite questions and answers using the prompts.**

1. hold my bag for a minute

   A: Would you hold my bag for a minute?

   B: Sure. No problem.

2. close the door

   A: ______________________________________________?

   B: ______________________________________________.

3. tell me where the bank is

   A: ______________________________________________?

   B: ______________________________________________.

4. turn the music down

   A: ______________________________________________?

   B: ______________________________________________.

5. take my letter to the post office

   A: ______________________________________________?

   B: ______________________________________________.

6. smoke outside please

   A: ______________________________________________?

   B: ______________________________________________.

7. drive for a while

   A: ______________________________________________?

   B: ______________________________________________.

## 12d The Imperative

Student Book p. 336

### 10 Practice

**Put these instructions in the correct order.**

**How to Send Email**

_____ Read the message before you send it.

_____ Click on the "Send" button.

_____ Write your message.

_____ Put your friend's email address in the "To" space.

### 11 Practice

**Put these instructions in the correct order.**

**How to Make Spaghetti**

_____ Put some salt in the water.

_____ Take the pasta out of the water.

_____ Cook for eight to ten minutes.

_____ Put water in a pot.

_____ Boil the water.

_____ Add tomatoes, garlic, and cheese.

_____ Put the spaghetti in the boiling water.

### 12 Practice

**Complete the sentences with affirmative or negative imperatives telling what people should and shouldn't do in the library.**

| | | | | |
|---|---|---|---|---|
| be | keep | put | talk | smoke |
| eat | make | return | throw away | use |

**1.** ____________________ cigarettes.

**2.** ____________________ quiet.

**3.** ____________________ food.

4. ____________________ loudly.

5. ____________________ cell phones.

6. ____________________ reservations to use the computers.

7. ____________________ books back on the shelf.

8. ____________________ library clean.

9. ____________________ your bottles and cans.

10. ____________________ books in three weeks.

## 13 Practice

**It's Jay's first day at his new job as a waiter. Complete the sentences with affirmative or negative imperatives telling him what to do and what not to do.**

be
close
stand
take
talk
wash
wear

1. ____________________ polite.

2. ____________________ your hands.

3. ____________________ the customers' orders.

4. ____________________ around with nothing to do.

5. ____________________ clean uniform.

6. ____________________ too much to customers.

7. ____________________ the door when you leave.

# SELF-TEST

**A Choose the best answer, A, B, C, or D, to complete the sentence. Mark your answer by darkening the oval with the same letter.**

**1.** _______ go down town tomorrow.

**A.** Could (A) (B) (C) (D)
**B.** Let's
**C.** Let
**D.** Would

**2.** _______ talk. The students are working.

**A.** Could (A) (B) (C) (D)
**B.** Would like
**C.** Don't
**D.** Would

**3.** I _______ to have more homework tonight.

**A.** wouldn't like (A) (B) (C) (D)
**B.** let's
**C.** could
**D.** would

**4.** What country would _______ to live in?

**A.** like (A) (B) (C) (D)
**B.** you like
**C.** let's
**D.** would

**5.** _______ your books to page 63.

**A.** Could you (A) (B) (C) (D)
**B.** Let's
**C.** Would you
**D.** Open

**6.** _______ give me some more time?

**A.** Could you to (A) (B) (C) (D)
**B.** Would you like
**C.** Let
**D.** Would you

**7.** Would they like to come to the beach with us? _______________

**A.** Yes, they do. (A) (B) (C) (D)
**B.** Yes, let's.
**C.** No, they wouldn't.
**D.** Yes, they wouldn't.

**8.** _______ leave at about 9:00.

**A.** Would you like (A) (B) (C) (D)
**B.** He
**C.** Let's
**D.** I would like

**9.** _______ do the dishes right now. We have to go.

**A.** Couldn't (A) (B) (C) (D)
**B.** Don't
**C.** Let not
**D.** Wouldn't

**10.** Could you please _______ my car?

**A.** to wash (A) (B) (C) (D)
**B.** washed
**C.** wash
**D.** washing

**B Find the underlined word or phrase, A, B, C, or D, that is incorrect. Mark your answer by darkening the oval with the same letter.**

1. Would (A) you to come (B) with us, or are you (C) too (D) busy?

   Ⓐ Ⓑ Ⓒ Ⓓ

2. Let (A) pick up (B) Jane before (C) we go (D) the party.

   Ⓐ Ⓑ Ⓒ Ⓓ

3. Don't (A) to be (B) late. We have to (C) be there in half an hour (D).

   Ⓐ Ⓑ Ⓒ Ⓓ

4. Let's (A) don't (B) play the movie right now. We can do (C) it after dinner (D).

   Ⓐ Ⓑ Ⓒ Ⓓ

5. Could you (A) please to close (B) the window? I'm (C) really cold (D).

   Ⓐ Ⓑ Ⓒ Ⓓ

6. The light (A) is red (B). Don't (C) to cross (D) the street.

   Ⓐ Ⓑ Ⓒ Ⓓ

7. Our teacher is giving (A) us (B) a test tomorrow. Let (C) study (D).

   Ⓐ Ⓑ Ⓒ Ⓓ

8. David would like (A) go with you if (B) you have (C) enough (D) room.

   Ⓐ Ⓑ Ⓒ Ⓓ

9. Frank would to (A) travel (B) to New York (C) for business (D).

   Ⓐ Ⓑ Ⓒ Ⓓ

10. To sit (A) down and be (B) quiet. People (C) are working (D).

   Ⓐ Ⓑ Ⓒ Ⓓ

# UNIT 13
# ADJECTIVES AND ADVERBS

## 13a Adjectives and Nouns Used as Adjectives

Student Book p. 346

### 1 Practice

**Identify the underlined words. Put an X beside *Noun* or *Adjective*.**

| | | Noun | Adjective |
|---|---|---|---|
| **1.** | Christina is a busy mom. | X | |
| **2.** | She has two young children. | | |
| **3.** | They are girls. | | |
| **4.** | Jasmine has blue eyes. | | |
| **5.** | Chloe has brown eyes. | | |
| **6.** | Christina has a full time job. | | |
| **7.** | Her job is interesting. | | |
| **8.** | She is a writer. | | |
| **9.** | She writes books on history. | | |
| **10.** | Sometimes, she writes love stories. | | |
| **11.** | Christina is very happy. | | |

### 2 Practice

**Identify the underlined words. Put an X beside *Noun* or *Adjective*.**

| | | Noun | Adjective |
|---|---|---|---|
| **1.** | Derek is a popular teacher. | | |
| **2.** | He enjoys his students. | | |
| **3.** | Some students are a little lazy. | | |
| **4.** | Some students don't like English. | | |
| **5.** | But Derek likes to work with those students. | | |
| **6.** | Derek is married. | | |
| **7.** | He has a beautiful baby girl. | | |
| **8.** | He and his wife bought a new house. | | |

9. The house is gray and white. Noun _____ Adjective _____

10. Derek has a good life. Noun _____ Adjective _____

## 3 Practice

**Underline the nouns used as adjectives. There are 12 nouns used as adjectives.**

Amanda is a high school student. She is waiting for the school bus near her house. She has a Spanish dictionary, a pencil case, and her gym shoes in her backpack. She doesn't want to be late for her English class. Today she has a history test and then after school, she is going to go to the drama club. On her lunch hour, she buys a sandwich and sits with her friends. There are juice cartons all over the table. The jazz band is playing for the students during lunch. She's going to get a job during her summer vacation.

## 4 Practice

**Underline the nouns used as adjectives. There are 10 nouns used as adjectives.**

Ed wanted to ride his bike downtown, but someone stole his bicycle seat! He had to walk. He met his girlfriend for lunch after her yoga class. When he crossed the street to the restaurant, he didn't see the street light and a car almost hit him! When he got to the sandwich shop, he ordered some fruit salad and a chocolate cookie.

After lunch, Ed and Marcia walked down the street looking in the store windows. They walked around the art museum for an hour, and then they went to Marcia's house. She has a big flower garden. They went into the garden. Marcia took a nap, and Ed read the afternoon newspaper.

## 5 Practice

**Look at the picture. Complete the names of the objects with words from the list.**

| breakfast | cereal | pepper | strawberry |
|---|---|---|---|
| butter | milk | salt | sugar |

1. ____milk____ carton
2. ______________ jam
3. ______________ knife
4. ______________ box
5. ______________ shaker
6. ______________ shaker
7. ______________ bowl
8. ______________ table

## 6 Practice

**Combine the word in capital letters with the words under it. You can put the word in front of or after the word in capital letters. Write the definition. Check your answers with your teacher or a dictionary.**

**1.** PAPER

hat ______________________________

towel ______________________________

wall ______________________________

**2.** TV

dinner ______________________________

tray ______________________________

color ______________________________

**3.** CAR

seat ______________________________

radio ______________________________

toy ______________________________

**4.** COFFEE

maker ______________________________

pot ______________________________

beans ______________________________

**5.** CAMERA

digital ______________________________

video ______________________________

case ______________________________

**6.** CLOTHES

hanger ______________________________

work ______________________________

rain ______________________________

7. HISTORY

art ______________________________

class ______________________________

teacher ______________________________

8. CAKE

birthday ______________________________

rice ______________________________

plate ______________________________

9. HAND

hour ______________________________

shake ______________________________

ball ______________________________

10. NIGHT

time ______________________________

Saturday ______________________________

light ______________________________

11. BOOK

note ______________________________

store ______________________________

match ______________________________

12. APPLE

juice ______________________________

pie ______________________________

sauce ______________________________

13. HOUSE

boat ______________________________

mate ______________________________

dog ______________________________

**14.** SALT

table ______________________________

shaker ______________________________

water ______________________________

**15.** WATCH

wrist ______________________________

digital ______________________________

stop ______________________________

**16.** TRUCK

driver ______________________________

stop ______________________________

garbage ______________________________

**17.** SHOE

store ______________________________

horse ______________________________

sale ______________________________

**18.** ROAD

work ______________________________

block ______________________________

dirt ______________________________

**19.** COMPUTER

desk ______________________________

screen ______________________________

chip ______________________________

**20.** PHONE

cell ______________________________

book ______________________________

number ______________________________

# 13b Word Order of Adjectives

Student Book p. 350

## 7 Practice

**Put the adjectives in the correct order.**

| | | | | |
|---|---|---|---|---|
| **1.** | paper/brown | a/an | brown paper | bag |
| **2.** | black and white/old | a/an | ________________ | TV |
| **3.** | plastic/cheap/white | a/an | ________________ | toy |
| **4.** | blue/ugly/old | a/an | ________________ | coat |
| **5.** | gray/cute/small | a/an | ________________ | dog |
| **6.** | metal/dirty/cold | a/an | ________________ | chair |
| **7.** | wooden/new/small | a/an | ________________ | desk |
| **8.** | long/boring | a/an | ________________ | exercise |
| **9.** | hot/delicious/chocolate | a/an | ________________ | cookie |
| **10.** | small/clean/green | a/an | ________________ | room |

## 8 Practice

**Put the adjectives in the correct order.**

| | | | | |
|---|---|---|---|---|
| **1.** | Italian/handsome/young | a/an | ________________ | man |
| **2.** | brown/comfortable/leather | a/an | ________________ | chair |
| **3.** | new/English/interesting | a/an | ________________ | movie |
| **4.** | narrow/dangerous/short | a/an | ________________ | street |
| **5.** | old/diamond/expensive | a/an | ________________ | necklace |
| **6.** | Chinese/old/nice | a/an | ________________ | woman |
| **7.** | Japanese/white/delicious | some | ________________ | rice |
| **8.** | cold/sunny | a/an | ________________ | morning |
| **9.** | cold/sweet | some | ________________ | ice cream |
| **10.** | medium/red/good | a/an | ________________ | apple |

## 9 Practice

**Complete the sentences with words from the list. Use each word once.**

| | | | |
|---|---|---|---|
| big | dining | nice | sunny |
| cheese | grocery | picnic | wooden |

Fernando and Sylvia live in a ____(1)____ one-bedroom apartment. The bedroom is clean, and the living room is ____(2)____. In the ____(3)____ room, there is a ____(4)____ table with chairs. On the balcony, they have a ____(5)____ table. Their apartment is near the ____(6)____ store. Right now, Fernando is having a ____(7)____ sandwich. They have a ____(8)____ life.

## 10 Practice

**Use two adjectives or nouns used as adjectives to describe these things.**

**1.** your room

*I have a small blue room*.

**2.** your school

____________________.

**3.** your bicycle

____________________.

**4.** your hair

____________________.

**5.** your parents

____________________.

**6.** your shirt

____________________.

**7.** your computer

____________________.

**8.** your best friend

____________________.

**9.** your favorite vacation

____________________.

10. your backpack

_______________________________________________.

11. your wallet

_______________________________________________.

12. your city

_______________________________________________.

# 13c *The Same (As)*, *Similar (To)*, and *Different (From)*

Student Book p. 353

## 11 Practice

**Complete the sentences with *the same (as)*, *similar (to)*, or *different (from)*. Your answers may vary.**

1. Life in the country is ____________________ life in the city.
2. Men are ____________________ women.
3. Fast food in the United States is ____________________ fast food in South America.
4. Teenagers in Japan are ____________________ teenagers in England.
5. Mothers everywhere are ____________________.
6. Weather in Brazil and weather in Argentina are ____________________.
7. Music from the 1960s is ____________________ music from 2000.
8. IBM computers and PCs are ____________________.
9. Nine-year-old children and ten-year-old children are ____________________.
10. People around the world are ____________________.

## 12 Practice

**Look at the photos. Then complete the sentences with *the same (as)*, *similar (to)*, or *different (from)*.**

**Photo A**

**Photo B**

1. Photo A is ____________________ photo B.
2. Photos A and B are ____________________.

**Photo C**

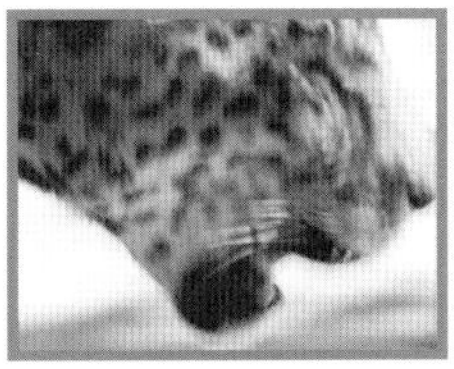

**Photo D**

3. Photo C is ______________________ photo D.

4. Photos C and D are ______________________.

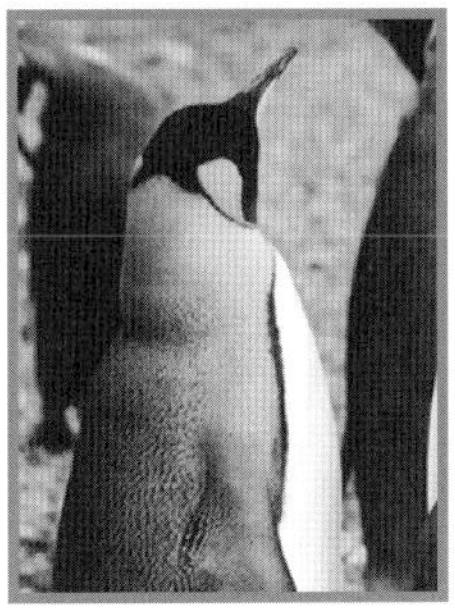

**Photo E**

**Photo F**

5. Photo E is ______________________ photo F.

6. Photos E and F are ______________________.

## 13 Practice

**Write about you and your family. Use *the same (as)*, *similar (to)*, or *different (from)*. Use the prompts or your own ideas.**

1. have/eyes

   *I have the same eyes as my dad*______________________.

2. enjoy/hobbies

   ______________________.

3. have/hair

   ______________________.

4. like/music

   ______________________.

5. be/height

   ______________________.

6. read/books

   ______________________.

# 13d *Like* and *Alike*

Student Book p. 355

## 14 Practice

**Complete the sentences with *like* or *alike*.**

1. Artie and Archie have similar names. Their names are ____alike____.
2. Artie and Archie have similar houses. Artie's house is ____________ Archie's house.
3. Artie and Archie have similar hobbies. Artie's hobbies are ____________ Archie's hobbies.
4. Artie and Archie have similar eyes. Their eyes are ____________.
5. Artie and Archie have similar gardens. Artie's garden is ____________ Archie's garden.
6. Artie and Archie went to similar universities. Artie's university is ____________ Archie's university.
7. Artie and Archie have similar furniture. Arties' furniture is ____________ Archie's furniture.
8. Artie and Archie buy similar books. Artie's books are ____________ Archie's books.
9. Artie and Archie have similar hair. Their hair is ____________.
10. Artie and Archie have similar digital cameras. Their cameras are ____________.
11. Artie and Archie have similar TVs. Their TVs are ____________.
12. Artie and Archie have similar children. Artie's children are ____________ Archie's children.
13. Artie and Archie bought similar computers. Artie's computer is ____________ Archie's computer.
14. Artie and Archie have similar cell phones. Their cell phones are ____________.
15. Artie and Archie have similar watches. Their watches are ____________.

## 15 Practice

**Which of these things are similar? Why? Use *like* or *alike* in your answers.**

| | | | |
|---|---|---|---|
| Austria | college | limes | shoes |
| cigarettes | cup | ocean | Switzerland |
| cigars | glass | sandals | university |
| clock | lemons | sea | watch |

1. Lemons are like limes. (OR) Lemons and limes are alike.
   They're both sour.
2. ______.
3. ______.
4. ______.
5. ______.
6. ______.
7. ______.
8. ______.

# 13e Comparative Form of Adjectives: *-er* and *More*

Student Book p. 357

## 16 Practice

**Write the comparative form of the adjectives.**

1. short shorter than
2. slim ______
3. tall ______
4. busy ______
5. good ______
6. heavy ______
7. early ______
8. handsome ______
9. friendly ______
10. old ______
11. nice ______
12. sweet ______
13. late ______
14. exciting ______
15. far ______
16. happy ______

## 17 Practice

**Write the comparative form of the adjectives.**

1. warm ______________
2. cool ______________
3. interesting ______________
4. loud ______________
5. shy ______________
6. large ______________
7. rich ______________
8. new ______________
9. fast ______________
10. modern ______________
11. quiet ______________
12. cheap ______________
13. easy ______________
14. bad ______________
15. serious ______________
16. delicious ______________

## 18 Practice

**Complete the sentences about the two restaurants. Use the comparative form of the adjectives in parentheses.**

| | Tom's Coffee Shack | Le Bon Mot |
|---|---|---|
| Dinner | \$10 – \$15 | \$25 – \$40 |
| Hours | 10:00 A.M. – 9:30 P.M. | 6:00 P.M. – 11:30 P.M. |
| Founded | 1998 | 1972 |
| Capacity | 45 people | 75 people |
| Food Rating | ★★ | ★★★ |

1. Tom's Coffee Shack is (cheap) *cheaper than* Le Bon Mot.
2. Le Bon Mot is (expensive) ______________ Tom's Coffee Shack.
3. Tom's is open (early) ______________ Le Bon Mot.
4. Le Bon Mot is open (late) ______________ Tom's.
5. Tom's is (new) ______________ Le Bon Mot.
6. Le Bon Mot is (big) ______________ Tom's.
7. Tom's is (small) ______________ Le Bon Mot.
8. Le Bon Mot is (old) ______________ Tom's.
9. The food at Le Bon Mot is (good) ______________ the food at Tom's Coffee Shack.

## 19 Practice

**Complete the sentences about the two movies. Use the comparative form of the adjectives in parentheses. Some information is provided.**

| | Battle Guns from Space | Love Sweet Love |
|---|---|---|
| Length | 120 minutes | 90 minutes |
| Story | Three brothers fight an evil space monster. | A young man and woman fall in love. |
| Rating | ★★★★ | ★★ |
| Year | 2003 | 2000 |

1. *Battle Guns from Space* is (long) ___longer than___ *Love Sweet Love.*
2. *Love Sweet Love* is (short) ______________ *Battle Guns from Space.*
3. *Battle Guns from Space* is (good) ______________ *Love Sweet Love.*
4. *Battle Guns from Space* is (exciting) ______________ *Love Sweet Love.*
5. *Battle Guns from Space* is (interesting) ______________ *Love Sweet Love.*
6. *Battle Guns from Space* is (new) ______________ *Love Sweet Love.*
7. *Love Sweet Love* is (old) ______________ *Battle Guns from Space.*
8. *Love Sweet Love* is (slow) ______________ *Battle Guns from Space*

## 20 Practice

**Complete the sentences about San Francisco and Tokyo. Use the comparative form of the adjectives in parentheses. Some information is provided.**

| San Francisco | | Tokyo | |
|---|---|---|---|
| Population: | 776,000 | Population: | 12,000,000 |
| Average temperature: | 40–70°F / 4–21°C | Average temperature: | 30–85 F° / -1–29°C |
| Rain: | 19.3 inches / 49 cm | Rain: | 60 inches / 152 cm |

1. Tokyo is (big) ___bigger than___ San Francisco.
2. San Francisco is (small) ______________ Tokyo.
3. Tokyo is (crowded) ______________ San Francisco.
4. Tokyo is (rainy) ______________ San Francisco.
5. San Francisco is (warm) ______________ Tokyo in the winter.
6. Tokyo is (cold) ______________ San Francisco in the winter.
7. Tokyo is (hot) ______________ San Francisco in the summer.
8. Tokyo is (expensive) ______________ San Francisco.

9. Tokyo is (exciting) ______________________ San Francisco.

10. Tokyo is (old) ______________________ San Francisco.

## 21 Practice

**Complete the sentences about Buenos Aires and Paris. Use the comparative form of the adjectives in parentheses. Some information is provided.**

| **Buenos Aires** | | **Paris** | |
|---|---|---|---|
| Population: | 12,400,000 | Population: | 2,000,000 |
| Average temperature: | 50–82°F / 5–29°C | Average temperature: | 37–65°F / 3–18°C |
| Rain: | 3.5 inches / 9 cm | Rain: | 22 inches / 57 cm |

1. Buenos Aires is (big) ______________________ Paris.
2. Paris is (rain) ______________________ Buenos Aires.
3. Buenos Aires is (warm) ______________________ Paris.
4. Paris is (far) ______________________ north ______________________ Buenos Aires.
5. Paris is (small) ______________________ Buenos Aires.
6. Buenos Aires is (dry) ______________________ Paris.
7. Paris is (cold) ______________________ Buenos Aires.
8. Buenos Aires is (far) ______________________ south ______________________ Paris.

## 22 Practice

**Write sentences about your life a year ago and now. Use comparative forms.**

1. tall — *I'm taller now than I was a year ago.*
2. intelligent ______________________
3. happy ______________________
4. busy ______________________
5. old ______________________
6. thin/heavy ______________________
7. shy/outgoing ______________________
8. my hair/long OR short ______________________
9. my classes/easy OR difficult ______________________

10. my English/good OR bad ______________________

11. (your own idea) ______________________

12. (your own idea) ______________________

# 13f *As* … *As*, *Not As* … *As*, and *Less* … *Than*

Student Book p. 360

## 23 Practice

**Complete the sentences with *as* … *as* and the adjectives in parentheses.**

1. Shannon's school is (big) _____as big as_____ Renaldo's school.
2. Shannon's school is (fun) ______________________ Renaldo's school.
3. Shannon's school is (quiet) ______________________ Renaldo's school.
4. Shannon's school is (modern) ______________________ Renaldo's school.
5. Shannon's teachers are (strict) ______________________ Renaldo's teachers.
6. Shannon's school is (clean) ______________________ Renaldo's school.
7. Shannon's classes are (interesting) ______________________ Renaldo's classes.

## 24 Practice

**Complete the sentences with *as* … *as* or *not as* … *as* and the adjectives in parentheses.**

1. Her computer is (not, fast) ______________________ mine.
2. Her computer is (not, new) ______________________ mine.
3. Judy's computer is (expensive) ______________________ mine.
4. My computer is (not, large) ______________________ hers.
5. My computer is (not, heavy) ______________________ hers.
6. Her computer is (easy) ______________________ mine.
7. Her computer is (good) ______________________ mine.

## 25 Practice

**Write the sentences to have the same meaning using *less*. Write "No change" if it isn't possible to use *less*.**

1. Yoko's street isn't as safe as Joe's street. No change.
2. Joe's street isn't as dangerous as Yoko's.
   Joe's street is less dangerous than Yoko's.
3. Yoko's house isn't as comfortable as Joe's house.
   ____________________.
4. Yoko's house isn't as far away as Joe's house.
   ____________________.
5. Joe isn't as happy as Yoko.
   ____________________.
6. Joe isn't as outgoing as Yoko.
   ____________________.
7. Yoko isn't as shy as Joe.
   ____________________.
8. Joe isn't as nice as Yoko.
   ____________________.
9. Joe's job isn't as flexible as Yoko's job.
   ____________________.
10. Yoko's job isn't as difficult as Joe's job.
    ____________________.
11. Yoko's class isn't as early as Joe's class.
    ____________________.
12. Joe's class isn't as interesting as Yoko's class.
    ____________________.
13. Yoko isn't as serious as Joe.
    ____________________.
14. Joe's lunch isn't as delicious as Yoko's lunch.
    ____________________.

## 26 Practice

**Many expressions use *as ... as*. Choose the word that best fits the expression. Use a dictionary if necessary.**

**1.** Her daughter is as good as ______________________.  **a.** silk

**2.** What's wrong? You're as white as a ______________________.  **b.** honey

**3.** The little boy is as quiet as a ______________________.  **c.** gold

**4.** Your hand is as smooth as ______________________.  **d.** mouse

**5.** That cake is as sweet as ______________________.  **e.** ghost

## 27 Practice

**Write *C* next to the expression if it is correct. Write *I* if the expression is incorrect. If the expression is incorrect, write the correct one.**

__I__ **1.** He's as busy as a picture.  He's as busy as a bee.

_____ **2.** She's as pretty as an ox.  ______________________

_____ **3.** That man is as strong as an ox.  ______________________

_____ **4.** I'm as hungry as a bear.  ______________________

_____ **5.** You're as cold as a beet.  ______________________

## 28 Practice

**Write sentences with the same meaning using *as ... as*.**

**1.** Vincenzo's Italian Restaurant is better than the Seaside Café.

The Seaside Café isn't as good as Vincenzo's Italian Restaurant.

**2.** Vincenzo's Italian Restaurant is more expensive than the Seaside Café.

______________________________________________.

**3.** The food at Vincenzo's Italian Restaurant is more delicious than the food at the Seaside Café. ______________________________________________

______________________________________________.

**4.** The Seaside Café is less luxurious than Vincenzo's Italian Restaurant.

______________________________________________.

**5.** Vincenzo's Italian Restaurant is larger than the Seaside Café.

______________________________________________.

6. The Seaside Café is dirtier than Vincenzo's Italian Restaurant.

______________________________________________.

7. Vincenzo's Italian Restaurant is newer than the Seaside Café.

______________________________________________.

8. Vincenzo's Italian Restaurant is fancier than the Seaside Café.

______________________________________________.

9. The music at the Seaside Café is louder than the music at Vincenzo's Italian Restaurant. ______________________________________________

______________________________________________.

10. The waiters at Vincenzo's Italian Restaurant are nicer than the waiters at the Seaside Café. ______________________________________________

______________________________________________.

## 29 Practice

**Write sentences with the same meaning using *as ... as*.**

1. Amy's apartment is cheaper than Jeff's house.

   *Jeff's house isn't as cheap as Amy's apartment*.
   (OR)
   *Amy's apartment isn't as expensive as Jeff's house*.

2. Jeff's house is bigger than Amy's apartment.

   ______________________________________________.

3. Amy's apartment is less comfortable than Jeff's house.

   ______________________________________________.

4. Jeff's house is quieter than Amy's apartment.

   ______________________________________________.

5. Amy's apartment is safer than Jeff's house.

   ______________________________________________.

6. Jeff's house is farther from the school than Amy's apartment.

   ______________________________________________.

7. Amy's apartment is less modern than Jeff's house.

   ______________________________________________.

8. Jeff's house is cleaner than Amy's apartment.

______________________________________________.

9. Amy's apartment is older than Jeff's house.

______________________________________________.

# 13g Superlative Form of Adjectives: *-est* and *Most*

Student Book p. 366

## 30 Practice

**Write the superlative form of the adjectives.**

| | | | |
|---|---|---|---|
| 1. short | the shortest | 9. friendly | ________ |
| 2. slim | ________ | 10. old | ________ |
| 3. tall | ________ | 11. nice | ________ |
| 4. busy | ________ | 12. sweet | ________ |
| 5. good | ________ | 13. late | ________ |
| 6. heavy | ________ | 14. exciting | ________ |
| 7. early | ________ | 15. far | ________ |
| 8. beautiful | ________ | 16. happy | ________ |

## 31 Practice

**Write the superlative form of the adjectives.**

| | | | |
|---|---|---|---|
| 1. warm | ________ | 9. fast | ________ |
| 2. cool | ________ | 10. modern | ________ |
| 3. difficult | ________ | 11. quiet | ________ |
| 4. loud | ________ | 12. cheap | ________ |
| 5. attractive | ________ | 13. easy | ________ |
| 6. large | ________ | 14. bad | ________ |
| 7. rich | ________ | 15. serious | ________ |
| 8. new | ________ | 16. interesting | ________ |

## 32 Practice

**Complete the sentences with the correct form of the adjectives in parentheses.**

1. Bristle cone pine tress are (old) *the* ____________ trees in the world.
2. Bee humming birds are (small) ____________ birds in the world.
3. Siberian tigers are (large) ____________ cats in the world.
4. The cheetah is (fast) ____________ land animal in the world.
5. Blue whales are (big) ____________ animals in the world.
6. Giraffes have (long) ____________ necks of all animals.
7. The rhinoceros beetle is (strong) ____________ animal in the world. It can carry 850 times its weight!
8. The lionfish is (beautiful) ____________ fish in the sea.

## 33 Practice

**Write sentences using the comparative or superlative and the information in the chart.**

| Robert | Clint | Buddy |
|---|---|---|
| 5'9" | 5'11" | 6'1" |
| 175 lbs | 190 lbs | 200 lbs |
| 24 years old | 32 years old | 40 years old |
| very outgoing | not shy | shy |
| takes classes part time | works and goes to school | has part-time job |
| smokes | exercises three days a week | exercises five days a week |
| eats fast food | | |

busy, healthy, heavy, old, outgoing, short, shy, tall, thin, young

1. *Buddy is the tallest* ____________.

2. Clint is taller than Robert.

3. ________________.

4. ________________.

5. ________________.

6. ________________.

7. ________________.

8. ________________.

9. ________________.

10. ________________.

11. ________________.

12. ________________.

13. ________________.

14. ________________.

15. ________________.

## 34 Practice

**Write answers to the following questions.**

1. Who is the tallest person in your class?

   ________________.

2. Who is the most intelligent person in your school?

   ________________.

3. What is the most popular place in your town?

   ________________.

4. What is the best restaurant in your town?

   ________________.

5. What was the worst day of your life?

   ________________.

6. Who is the friendliest person you know?

   ________________.

7. What was the best day of your life?

_______________________________________________.

8. Who is the funniest person in your family?

_______________________________________________.

9. What was the most difficult class you had last year?

_______________________________________________.

10. What's the tallest building in your town?

_______________________________________________.

## 35 Practice

**Write *C* next to the sentence if the superlative is used correctly. Write *I* if the superlative is used incorrectly. If the superlative is incorrect, write the correct one.**

_____ 1. Mt. Everest is the tallest mountain in the world.

_____ 2. Gabriella was the most prettiest girl at the party.

_____ 3. Sam's apartment is the most cheap.

_____ 4. What was the most important day of your life?

_____ 5. That's the best store in the mall.

_____ 6. Todd lives the farest away.

_____ 7. Valerie is the nicest person I know.

_____ 8. Arturo gets up the most early.

1. *No change*.
2. *Gabriella was the prettiest girl at the party*.
3. _______________________________________________.
4. _______________________________________________.
5. _______________________________________________.
6. _______________________________________________.
7. _______________________________________________.
8. _______________________________________________.

# 13h *One Of The* + Superlative + Plural Noun

Student Book p. 370

## 36 Practice

**Write sentences using the "*one of the* + superlative + plural noun" pattern.**

1. Sahara Desert/hot place/the earth

   The Sahara Desert is one of the hottest places on the earth.

2. Empire State Building/tall building/New York City

   ______________________________.

3. The Amazon River/old river/the world

   ______________________________.

4. Mexico City/crowded city/the world

   ______________________________.

5. rice/important food/Asia

   ______________________________.

6. *The Matrix*/popular film/ever

   ______________________________.

7. chile peppers/spicy ingredient/a burrito

   ______________________________.

8. The Great Wall of China/long wall/ever built

   ______________________________.

9. ice cream/cold dessert/the menu

   ______________________________.

10. The Eiffel Tower/famous structure/Europe

    ______________________________.

## 37 Practice

**Write questions and answers using the "*one of the* + superlative + plural noun" pattern.**

1. tall/people/in your class

   Who is one of the tallest people in your class ?

   Jennifer is one of the tallest people in our class .

2. nice/people/in your class

   ______________________________?

   ______________________________.

3. intelligent/people/you know

   ______________________________?

   ______________________________.

4. famous/place/in your town

   ______________________________?

   ______________________________.

5. good/restaurant/in your town

   ______________________________?

   ______________________________.

6. great/musician/in jazz

   ______________________________?

   ______________________________.

7. good/book/you have read

   ______________________________?

   ______________________________.

8. tall/building/in your town

   ______________________________?

   ______________________________.

9. interesting/subjects/in school

   ______________________________?

   ______________________________.

**10.** famous/person/your country

_______________________________________________?

_______________________________________________.

**11.** expensive/thing/you have

_______________________________________________?

_______________________________________________.

**12.** happy/day/in your life

_______________________________________________?

_______________________________________________.

**13.** good/place/for teenagers/in your town

_______________________________________________?

_______________________________________________.

**14.** bad/movie/you saw last year

_______________________________________________?

_______________________________________________.

# 13i Adjectives and Adverbs

Student Book p. 372

## 38 Practice

**Write the words from the list in the correct columns.**

| | | | | |
|---|---|---|---|---|
| bad | easily | hard | rainy | softly |
| clean | expensive | hardly | sad | sweetly |
| crowded | fast | interesting | salty | warmly |
| differently | fluently | late | small | well |
| dirty | good | quickly | | |

| Adjective | Adverb | Adjective or Adverb |
|---|---|---|
| *bad* | | |
| | | |
| | | |
| | | |
| | | |
| | | |
| | | |

## 39 Practice

**Underline the correct form of the adjective or adverb.**

1. Carlos plays guitar (good / well).
2. He's a (good / well) guitar player.
3. His bedroom is (dirty / dirtily).
4. We did the homework (easy / easily).
5. The homework was (easy / easily).
6. I love you (deep / deeply).
7. It was (bad / badly) news.
8. She gave me the news (nice / nicely).
9. She speaks Spanish (beautiful / beautifully).
10. Her Spanish is (beautiful / beautifully).
11. That pizza was (salty / saltily).
12. Drive (careful / carefully).
13. This is a (heavy / heavily) book.
14. Yes, but it's (interesting / interestingly).
15. Kathy's kitchen is (modern / modernly).
16. My bed isn't (comfortable / comfortably).
17. I sleep (comfortable / comfortably).
18. We drank the lemonade (thirsty / thirstily).
19. We were (thirsty / thirstily).
20. Lauren answered the question (quiet / quietly).
21. She's a (quiet / quietly) person.
22. Those shoes were (cheap / cheaply).
23. It's (hot / hotly)!
24. Bernice is a (careful / carefully) driver.

## 40 Practice

**Underline the correct form of the adjective or adverb.**

1. The flowers are growing (fast / fastly).
2. We got to class (late / lately).
3. Our teacher wasn't (happy / happily).
4. Erin finished the race (easy / easily).
5. It was an (easy / easily) race.
6. Jason went home (sad / sadly).
7. He was (sad / sadly).
8. Donovan is (busy / busily).
9. They arrived home (safe / safely).
10. Their neighborhood isn't (safe / safely).
11. (Happy / Happily) birthday!
12. The party was a lot of (fun / funnily).

## 41 Practice

**Write *C* next to the sentence if the adjective or adverb is used correctly. Write *I* if the adjective or adverb is used incorrectly.**

__C__ 1. This is a good book!

_____ 2. David drives too slow.

_____ 3. Their parents arrived home early.

_____ 4. He cooks good.

_____ 5. Gabe speaks German fluently.

_____ 6. Hiro is a good tennis player.

_____ 7. This room is very clean.

_____ 8. I sing bad.

_____ 9. Nelson came in the room quiet.

## 42 Practice

**Use adverbs to talk about how you do the following actions.**

| | | | |
|---|---|---|---|
| cook | draw | play sports | take photos |
| dance | drive | speak English | talk |
| do math | play piano | study | work |

1. I cook frequently.
2. ______________________.
3. ______________________.
4. ______________________.

5. ______________________________.

6. ______________________________.

7. ______________________________.

8. ______________________________.

9. ______________________________.

10. ______________________________.

11. ______________________________.

12. ______________________________.

## 13j Comparative and Superlative Forms of Adverbs

Student Book p. 375

### 43 Practice

**Complete the sentences using the comparative form of the underlined adverbs.**

1. Kathy speaks English fluently, but Sue *speaks it more fluently*.
2. Kathy works carefully, but Sue ______________________.
3. Sue drives slowly, but Kathy ______________________.
4. Sue discusses politics intelligently, but Kathy ______________________.
5. Kathy finished the test quickly, but Sue ______________________.
6. Kathy plays piano well, but Sue ______________________.
7. Sue speaks politely with customers, but Kathy ______________________.
8. Kathy runs fast, but Sue ______________________.
9. Sue did the job easily, but Kathy ______________________.
10. Kathy gets to work early, but Sue ______________________.

### 44 Practice

**Write sentences using the comparative form of adverbs in the list or your own.**

| beautifully | early | friendly | quickly |
|---|---|---|---|
| carefully | frequently | hard | well |

1. *Sharon paints beautifully, but Paco paints more beautifully.*
2. ______________________________.

3. ______________________________.

4. ______________________________.

5. ______________________________.

6. ______________________________.

7. ______________________________.

8. ______________________________.

## 45 Practice

**Read the descriptions of three new cars. Use adjectives and adverbs from the list to write sentences with comparatives and superlatives.**

big/small
cheap/expensive
clean/dirty
fast/slow
quickly/slowly
rough/smooth
safe/dangerous
well/bad

| The Eco | The Tank | The Splendor |
|---|---|---|
| 30 mi./gal | 10 mi./gal | 25 mi./gal |
| 2 passengers | 8 passengers | 5 passengers |
| top speed: 75 mph | top speed: 60 mph | top speed: 100 mph |
| $10,000 | $75,000 | $45,000 |
| good for the environment | bad for the air | causes a little air pollution |
| safety rating – ★★★ | safety rating – ★★ | safety rating – ★★★★★ |
| handles well | hard to handle | handles okay |
| drives roughly | drives okay | drives smoothly |

1. *The Eco handles the best*.

2. ______________________________.

3. ______________________________.

4. ______________________________.

5. ______________________________.

6. ______________________________.

7. ______________________________.

8. ______________________________.

9. ______________________________.

10. ______________________________.

# 13k *As* … *As* with Adverbs

Student Book p. 378

## 46 Practice

**Write sentences using *as* … *as* and information from the chart about Justin and Al.**

| Justin | Al |
|---|---|
| gets up at 5:50 A.M. | gets up at 9:00 A.M. |
| not good at sports | good at sports |
| works quickly | doesn't work quickly |
| doesn't speak French well | speaks French fluently |
| goes to bed at 11:00 P.M. | goes to bed at 3:00 A.M. |
| good cook | doesn't cook well |
| does well in school | doesn't do well in School |

1. *Justin doesn't play sports as well as Al does*.
2. ______________________________.
3. ______________________________.
4. ______________________________.
5. ______________________________.
6. ______________________________.
7. ______________________________.
8. ______________________________.
9. ______________________________.
10. ______________________________.
11. ______________________________.
12. ______________________________.

## 47 Practice

**Diane has a job interview tomorrow. Her father is giving her advice. Write sentences using *as* … *as* + *you can*.**

1. arrive/early

   *Arrive as early as you can*.

2. sleep/good/the night before

   ______________________________.

3. dress/neatly

_______________________________________________.

4. answer the questions/well

_______________________________________________.

5. listen to the questions/carefully

_______________________________________________.

6. thank them/nicely

_______________________________________________.

7. write a thank you note/soon

_______________________________________________.

## 48 Practice

**Write about events in your life using *as ... as + could*. Use adverbs from the list and your own.**

carefully    hard    well
fast    quickly

1. Last year, I studied for my exams as hard as I could.
2. _______________________________________________
_______________________________________________.
3. _______________________________________________
_______________________________________________.
4. _______________________________________________
_______________________________________________.
5. _______________________________________________
_______________________________________________.
6. _______________________________________________
_______________________________________________.
7. _______________________________________________
_______________________________________________.

# SELF-TEST

**A Choose the best answer, A, B, C, or D, to complete the sentence. Mark your answer by darkening the oval with the same letter.**

**1.** My mother has a ________ handbag.

**A.** beautiful old red (A) (B) (C) (D)
**B.** old red beautiful
**C.** red beautiful old
**D.** beautiful red old

**2.** Jefferson finished the work ________.

**A.** fastly (A) (B) (C) (D)
**B.** fast
**C.** quick
**D.** slow

**3.** Becky is ________ girl in the class.

**A.** more intelligent (A) (B) (C) (D)
**B.** most intelligent
**C.** the more intelligent
**D.** the most intelligent

**4.** Janice's apartment is ________ mine.

**A.** more cheaply (A) (B) (C) (D)
**B.** cheaper than
**C.** more cheaper
**D.** the cheapest than

**5.** Ann isn't ________ Sheila.

**A.** the same than (A) (B) (C) (D)
**B.** as popular than
**C.** as popular as
**D.** different

**6.** Look at the ________ car.

**A.** dirty blue old (A) (B) (C) (D)
**B.** old dirty blue
**C.** old blue dirty
**D.** dirty old blue

**7.** My sister's eyes are ________ my mother's.

**A.** the same as (A) (B) (C) (D)
**B.** the same
**C.** the same than
**D.** same as

**8.** Joanne is ________ Katie.

**A.** more heavy than (A) (B) (C) (D)
**B.** heavier than
**C.** as heavier as
**D.** heavy than

**9.** Joyce doesn't play piano ________ Irv.

**A.** as good as (A) (B) (C) (D)
**B.** the best
**C.** as well as
**D.** better

**10.** Osaka is ________ in Japan.

**A.** one of the nicest cities (A) (B) (C) (D)
**B.** nicer city than
**C.** one of the nicest city
**D.** one of the nicest

**B Find the underlined word or phrase, A, B, C, or D, that is incorrect. Mark your answer by darkening the oval with the same letter.**

1. Yellowstone <u>is the</u>(A) <u>older</u>(B) <u>national park</u>(C) in the United States.

   Ⓐ Ⓑ Ⓒ Ⓓ

2. <u>Jason is</u>(A) <u>alike</u>(B) his brother John. <u>They are</u>(C) very <u>polite</u>(D).

   Ⓐ Ⓑ Ⓒ Ⓓ

3. <u>Don't write</u>(A) on the <u>white small</u>(B) <u>piece of paper</u>(C) <u>on your desk</u>(D).

   Ⓐ Ⓑ Ⓒ Ⓓ

4. <u>Yesterday</u>(A) <u>was hot</u>(B), but today was one of the hottest day <u>of the year</u>(D).

   Ⓐ Ⓑ Ⓒ Ⓓ

5. <u>Our last house was</u>(A) <u>more</u>(B) <u>better</u>(C) <u>than</u>(D) the one we live in now.

   Ⓐ Ⓑ Ⓒ Ⓓ

6. Rodney's town is similar <u>like</u>(A) Gilberto's town, but <u>Gilberto's house is</u>(B) <u>bigger than</u>(C) <u>Rodney's</u>(D).

   Ⓐ Ⓑ Ⓒ Ⓓ

7. <u>Therese finished</u>(A) the race <u>more quick</u>(B) <u>than</u>(C) the <u>other women</u>(D).

   Ⓐ Ⓑ Ⓒ Ⓓ

8. <u>Life in the 1900s</u>(A) <u>was very</u>(B) <u>different</u>(C) <u>than</u>(D) life today.

   Ⓐ Ⓑ Ⓒ Ⓓ

9. Please drive as <u>carefully</u>(A) <u>than</u>(B) <u>you can</u>(C). The traffic is <u>heavy</u>(D) today.

   Ⓐ Ⓑ Ⓒ Ⓓ

10. Eun Ji worked <u>as</u>(A) <u>quick</u>(B) as she <u>could</u>(C), but she <u>didn't finish</u>(D) the test.

   Ⓐ Ⓑ Ⓒ Ⓓ

# UNIT 14
# THE PRESENT PERFECT

## 14a The Present Perfect of *Be: For* and *Since*

Student Book p. 388

### 1 Practice

**Complete the sentences with the present perfect of the verb *be*. You may use contractions.**

1. Mei came to this country six years ago. She *has been / 's been* here for six years.
2. Mei met Lin three years ago. They ____________________ friends for three years.
3. Mei and Lin moved into their apartment last August. They ____________________ in their apartment since August.
4. Mei became a nurse in 2003. She ____________________ a nurse since 2003.
5. Lin started school last September. She ____________________ a student since last September.
6. Lin caught a cold last Monday. She ____________________ sick since last Monday.
7. Mei started working a lot six weeks ago. She ____________________ very busy for six weeks.
8. Mei didn't eat breakfast this morning. She ____________________ hungry since this morning.
9. Lin met her boyfriend a year ago. She ____________________ with her boyfriend for a year.
10. Mei and Lin are happy. They ____________________ happy since they met each other.

## 2 Practice

**Complete the sentences with the present perfect of the verb *be*. You may use contractions.**

1. Gerald married Carol 25 years ago. They *'ve been / have been* married for 25 years.
2. He became a doctor many years ago. He ________________ a doctor for many years.
3. Carol quit her job last year. She (not) ________________ at her job since last year.
4. Carol became interested in gardening 15 years ago. She ________________ interested in gardening for 15 years.
5. Carol was very sick last summer. She (not) ________________ sick since last summer.
6. They moved to Hawaii last January. They ________________ in Hawaii since last January.
7. Their daughter had a baby six months ago. They ________________ grandparents for six months.
8. Gerald and Carol started to build a new house last month. They ________________ busy since last month.

## 3 Practice

**Write *for* or *since* in the blanks.**

1. ___*since*___ last week
2. ___*for*___ 30 minutes
3. ____________ 1999
4. ____________ one month
5. ____________ five years
6. ____________ 11:00
7. ____________ Tuesday
8. ____________ last Thursday
9. ____________ two days
10. ____________ January
11. ____________ 2002
12. ____________ two weeks
13. ____________ last night
14. ____________ half an hour
15. ____________ 9:00 this morning
16. ____________ midnight
17. ____________ one year
18. ____________ 15 weeks
19. ____________ this afternoon
20. ____________ a few months

## 4 Practice

**Read the following information. Write sentences using the present perfect of the verb *be*.**

1. Jose and Angela moved to Los Angeles in 2001.
   Jose and Angela have been in Los Angeles since 2001.
2. They had a baby in 2002.
   ______________________________.
3. Jose became interested in architecture five years ago.
   ______________________________.
4. Jose started school last year.
   ______________________________.
5. Angela became a bus driver a year and a half ago.
   ______________________________.
6. They moved in with Angela's parents a few months ago.
   ______________________________.

## 5 Practice

**Complete the sentences with the present perfect of the verb *be*. Use ideas from the list or your own.**

| | | | |
|---|---|---|---|
| a good place to visit | busy | happy | sleeping well |
| an English student | famous | married | studying English |

1. The singer Marc Anthony has been very famous for six years.
2. My country ______________ for ______________.
3. My best friend ______________ since ______________.
4. My best friend ______________ for ______________.
5. I ______________ since ______________.
6. My parents ______________ for ______________.
7. My family ______________ since ______________.
8. I ______________ interested in ______________ since ______________.
9. I (not) ______________ since ______________.
10. I (not) ______________ for ______________.

# 14b The Present Perfect: Regular and Irregular Verbs

Student Book p. 393

## 6 Practice

**Complete the chart with the correct forms of the verbs.**

| Base Form | Simple Past | Past Participle |
|---|---|---|
| 1. *make* | *made* | *made* |
| 2. | *had* | |
| 3. | *wrote* | |
| 4. | | *spoken* |
| 5. *read* | | |
| 6. | *called* | |
| 7. | | *studied* |
| 8. *be* | | |
| 9. | | *visited* |
| 10. | *knew* | |
| 11. | | *gone* |

## 7 Practice

**Read about Laura and Tina. Then write sentences about the story using the present perfect tense.**

Laura

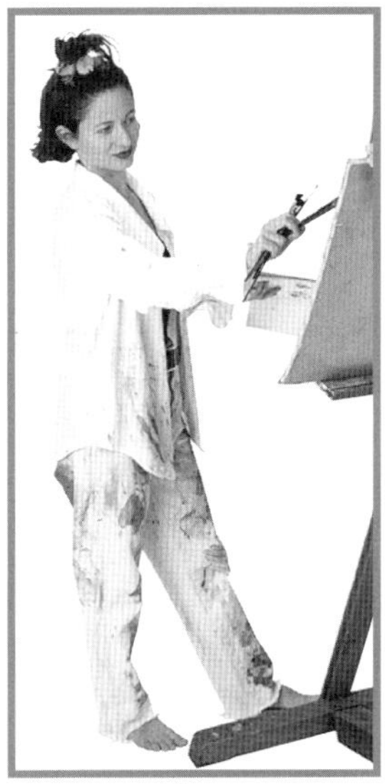

Tina

Laura and Tina are sisters, but their lives are very different. They grew up in New York City and Laura lives there now. Laura went to college and graduated in 2000. She is a doctor. Laura got married last year. She and her husband Terry had a baby six months ago. They moved into their house last spring.

Tina did not go to college. She left New York after high school and went to Florida. She became a full-time artist when she moved to Florida. Tina started selling paintings six months ago, and now she is selling a lot of them. Tina and her two cats moved into their loft three years ago. The last time Tina saw Laura was nine years ago. Laura is going to visit Tina in Florida for the first time this fall.

1. Laura/live/in New York all her life

Laura has lived in New York all her life.

2. Tina/live/Florida/high school

______________________________.

3. Laura/be/doctor/2000

______________________________.

4. Laura/be/married/last year

______________________________.

5. Tina/not see/Laura/nine years

______________________________.

6. Tina and her cats/live/loft/three years

______________________________.

7. Terry and Laura/be/parents/six months

______________________________.

8. They/live/house/last spring

______________________________.

9. Tina/work/artist/nine years

______________________________.

10. Tina/sell/paintings/six months

______________________________.

# 14c The Present Perfect: Negative Statements and Questions

Student Book p. 397

## 8 Practice

**Complete the questions and answers with the present perfect tense of the verbs in parentheses. You may use short answers.**

1. A: (you, go) Have you gone to the store?

   B: No, I ______________. I'll go now.

2. Henry (know) ______________________ Julia since they were children. They (be) ______________________ friends for a long time.

3. A: How long (have) ______________________ Susan ______________________ her dog?

   B: She (have) ______________________ him for nine years.

4. A: I (not, write) ______________________ any email this morning.

   B: Really? You ______________________?

   A: Really. I (be) ______________________ very busy.

5. A: How long (own) ______________________ Mr. Travis ______________________ his store?

   B: He (own) ______________________ it for 25 years.

   A: How long (know) ______________________ you ______________________ him?

   B: I (know) ______________________ him all my life! He's my grandfather.

6. A: (see) ______________________ you ______________________ my homework?

   B: Yes, I ______________________. It's on the table.

7. A: (send) ______________________ you ______________________ the mail?

   B: No, ______________________. I forgot. Sorry.

8. A: I'm hungry. (make) ______________________ you ______________________ lunch?

   B: Yes, I ______________________.

9. A: How long (speak) ______________________ Peter ______________________ German?

   B: I don't know. I know he (study) ______________________ it for many years.

10. A: How long (play) ______________________ your son ______________________ soccer?

   B: He (play) ______________________ soccer for a year, but he (be) ______________________ more interested in tennis lately.

## 9 Practice

**Complete the sentences with the present perfect tense of the verbs in parentheses. You may use short answers. Pay attention to the word order in questions.**

**A. An interviewer is talking to a famous singer.**

Interviewer: How long (you, want) have you wanted (1) to be a singer?

Singer: I (know) ______ (2) that I wanted to sing since I was a child.

Interviewer: Now you are famous. (change) ______ (3) this ______ (3) your life?

Singer: Yes, I (be) ______ (4) lucky. I (travel) ______ (5) to many countries, and I (have) ______ (6) a very good time.

Interviewer: So what are you doing now?

Singer: Well, I (write) ______ (7) some new songs, and I (be) ______ (8) very busy.

**B. Cho is talking to his English teacher.**

Cho: How long (you, be) ______ (1) an English teacher?

David Brown: I (be) ______ (2) a teacher for ten years.

Cho: How long (you, live) ______ (3) in Korea?

David Brown: We (be) ______ (4) in Seoul for a few months. My wife is from Korea. She (not, speak) ______ (5) Korean since she was a young girl.

Cho: (you, visit) ______ (6) other cities in Korea?

David Brown: Yes, we (travel) ______ (7) to many places. We (be) ______ (8) very happy.

**C. Betty is in another country but she's very lonely.**

Gloria: (you, make) ______(1)______ friends here?

Betty: No, I ______(2)______.

Gloria: You should. (you, call) ______(3)______ your parents?

Betty: Yes, I ______(4)______, but they weren't home.

Gloria: (you, write) ______(5)______ your friends?

Betty: Yes, but they (not, write) ______(6)______ me back.

**D. Luanne and Robert are on their first date.**

Luanne: How long (you, live) ______(1)______ here?

Richard: I (live) ______(2)______ here for five years. And you?

Luanne: I (live) ______(3)______ here for one year. How long (you, be) ______(4)______ an artist?

Richard: I (study) ______(5)______ art for many years, but I (not, make) ______(6)______ a lot of money as an artist yet.

## 14d The Present Perfect Tense: *Ever* and *Never*

Student Book p. 400

### 10 Practice

**Write *C* next to the sentence if *ever* or *never* is used correctly. Write *I* if *ever* or *never* is used incorrectly.**

__I__ **1.** I've ever seen that movie.

_____ **2.** Will has never had a motorcycle.

_____ **3.** Have you ever been to Thailand?

_____ **4.** Carrie has ever worked for that company for eight years.

_____ **5.** Tim hasn't never gone to that store.

______ **6.** How long have you ever been here?

______ **7.** Has Alice ever written a book?

______ **8.** She has never written a book.

______ **9.** Has Hugo ever traveled to Venezuela?

______ **10.** Joshua has ever made many friends here.

## II Practice

**Read the story about Fran. Then write questions and answers about Fran using *ever*, *never*, and the present perfect tense.**

Fran has lived in Los Angeles her whole life. She has a big family and loves living in California. She has never been to another country, and she has lived in the same house for 20 years. She loves going to movies and art museums. She is a good cook. She sometimes makes dinner for her friends. Fran is a writer and she works at home. She has many friends.

**1.** Fran/live/a different town

Has Fran ever lived in a different town ______?

No, she has never lived in a different town ______. (OR)

No, she hasn't ______.

**2.** Fran/be/another country

______?

______.

**3.** Fran/live/another city

______?

______.

**4.** Fran/write/anything

______?

______.

5. Fran/make friends

______________________________________________?

______________________________________________.

6. She/make/dinner for her friends

______________________________________________?

______________________________________________.

7. She/go/the movie theater

______________________________________________?

______________________________________________.

8. She/be/an art museum

______________________________________________?

______________________________________________.

## 12 Practice

**Write questions and affirmative and negative answers. Use *ever*, *never*, and the present perfect tense.**

1. you/make/pizza

Have you ever made pizza?

Yes, I have. I make pizza every month. (OR)

No, I've never made a pizza.

2. you/see/movie in English

______________________________________________?

______________________________________________.

3. you/be/on TV

______________________________________________?

______________________________________________.

4. you/live/in another country

______________________________________________?

______________________________________________.

5. you/fly/in a helicopter

____________________________________________________________?

____________________________________________________________.

6. you/ride/horses

____________________________________________________________?

____________________________________________________________.

7. your family/go on vacation/in Europe

____________________________________________________________?

____________________________________________________________.

8. you/color/your hair

____________________________________________________________?

____________________________________________________________.

9. your best friend/have/a party

____________________________________________________________?

____________________________________________________________.

10. you/be/very sick

____________________________________________________________?

____________________________________________________________.

11. you/have/a very bad day

____________________________________________________________?

____________________________________________________________.

12. you/drive/a truck

____________________________________________________________?

____________________________________________________________.

# SELF-TEST

**A Choose the best answer, A, B, C, or D, to complete the sentence. Mark your answer by darkening the oval with the same letter.**

**1.** They have been friends __________ two years.

**A.** since Ⓐ Ⓑ Ⓒ Ⓓ
**B.** ever
**C.** for
**D.** never

**2.** Has Fernando __________ been to Mexico?

**A.** since Ⓐ Ⓑ Ⓒ Ⓓ
**B.** ever
**C.** for
**D.** never

**3.** Have you ever __________ to Egypt?

**A.** goes Ⓐ Ⓑ Ⓒ Ⓓ
**B.** went
**C.** go
**D.** gone

**4.** Liu has __________ been to Hawaii.

**A.** since Ⓐ Ⓑ Ⓒ Ⓓ
**B.** ever
**C.** for
**D.** never

**5.** Cheryl and Rigo have been married __________ May.

**A.** since Ⓐ Ⓑ Ⓒ Ⓓ
**B.** ever
**C.** for
**D.** never

**6.** I've never __________ a bigger car.

**A.** haven't seen Ⓐ Ⓑ Ⓒ Ⓓ
**B.** saw
**C.** see
**D.** seen

**7.** Kenichi has been a chemist __________ last year.

**A.** since Ⓐ Ⓑ Ⓒ Ⓓ
**B.** ever
**C.** for
**D.** never

**8.** How long have you __________ here?

**A.** worked Ⓐ Ⓑ Ⓒ Ⓓ
**B.** ever worked
**C.** work
**D.** never

**9.** Jasmine has been a teacher __________ many years.

**A.** since Ⓐ Ⓑ Ⓒ Ⓓ
**B.** ever
**C.** for
**D.** never

**10.** I haven't __________ Spanish for 15 years.

**A.** never spoken Ⓐ Ⓑ Ⓒ Ⓓ
**B.** spoke
**C.** speak
**D.** spoken

**B Find the underlined word or phrase, A, B, C, or D, that is incorrect. Mark your answer by darkening the oval with the same letter.**

**1.** $\underline{\text{They}}_{\text{A}}$ $\underline{\text{have live}}_{\text{B}}$ in the apartment $\underline{\text{for}}_{\text{C}}$ only $\underline{\text{three weeks}}_{\text{D}}$.

Ⓐ Ⓑ Ⓒ Ⓓ

**2.** Diego has $\underline{\text{ever}}_{\text{A}}$ $\underline{\text{studied}}_{\text{B}}$ English $\underline{\text{since}}_{\text{C}}$ $\underline{\text{he was}}_{\text{D}}$ a high school student.

Ⓐ Ⓑ Ⓒ Ⓓ

**3.** $\underline{\text{He}}_{\text{A}}$ $\underline{\text{has owned}}_{\text{B}}$ $\underline{\text{the store}}_{\text{C}}$ $\underline{\text{since}}_{\text{D}}$ 22 years.

Ⓐ Ⓑ Ⓒ Ⓓ

**4.** $\underline{\text{How long}}_{\text{A}}$ $\underline{\text{has you}}_{\text{B}}$ $\underline{\text{been}}_{\text{C}}$ a computer programmer?

Ⓐ Ⓑ Ⓒ Ⓓ

**5.** My parents $\underline{\text{have}}_{\text{A}}$ $\underline{\text{ever}}_{\text{B}}$ $\underline{\text{been}}_{\text{C}}$ to Paris. They $\underline{\text{loved}}_{\text{D}}$ it.

Ⓐ Ⓑ Ⓒ Ⓓ

**6.** $\underline{\text{Paul and Andrea}}_{\text{A}}$ $\underline{\text{have}}_{\text{B}}$ $\underline{\text{never}}_{\text{C}}$ $\underline{\text{went}}_{\text{D}}$ to India.

Ⓐ Ⓑ Ⓒ Ⓓ

**7.** $\underline{\text{How long}}_{\text{A}}$ $\underline{\text{has your mother}}_{\text{B}}$ $\underline{\text{ever}}_{\text{C}}$ $\underline{\text{worked}}_{\text{D}}$ for that company?

Ⓐ Ⓑ Ⓒ Ⓓ

**8.** Yumiko hasn't $\underline{\text{never}}_{\text{A}}$ $\underline{\text{worked}}_{\text{B}}$ for that company $\underline{\text{since}}_{\text{C}}$ $\underline{\text{1999}}_{\text{D}}$.

Ⓐ Ⓑ Ⓒ Ⓓ

**9.** Chuck $\underline{\text{has}}_{\text{A}}$ $\underline{\text{been}}_{\text{B}}$ at school $\underline{\text{for}}_{\text{C}}$ 9:00 $\underline{\text{this morning}}_{\text{D}}$.

Ⓐ Ⓑ Ⓒ Ⓓ

**10.** Young Ji hasn't $\underline{\text{never}}_{\text{A}}$ $\underline{\text{been}}_{\text{B}}$ home $\underline{\text{since}}_{\text{C}}$ $\underline{\text{last Saturday}}_{\text{D}}$.

Ⓐ Ⓑ Ⓒ Ⓓ